SAINT DOMINIC

BOOKS BY MARY FABYAN WINDEATT

A Series of Twenty Books

Stories of the Saints for Young People ages 10 to 100

THE CHILDREN OF FATIMA
And Our Lady's Message to the World

THE CURÉ OF ARS
The Story of St. John Vianney, Patron Saint of Parish Priests

THE LITTLE FLOWER
The Story of St. Therese of the Child Jesus

PATRON SAINT OF FIRST COMMUNICANTS
The Story of Blessed Imelda Lambertini

THE MIRACULOUS MEDAL
The Story of Our Lady's Appearances to St. Catherine Labouré

ST. LOUIS DE MONTFORT
The Story of Our Lady's Slave, St. Louis Mary Grignion De Montfort

SAINT THOMAS AQUINAS
The Story of "The Dumb Ox"

SAINT CATHERINE OF SIENA
The Story of the Girl Who Saw Saints in the Sky

SAINT HYACINTH OF POLAND
The Story of the Apostle of the North

SAINT MARTIN DE PORRES
The Story of the Little Doctor of Lima, Peru

SAINT ROSE OF LIMA
The Story of the First Canonized Saint of the Americas

PAULINE JARICOT
Foundress of the Living Rosary & The Society for the Propagation of the Faith

SAINT DOMINIC
Preacher of the Rosary and Founder of the Dominican Order

SAINT PAUL THE APOSTLE
The Story of the Apostle to the Gentiles

SAINT BENEDICT
The Story of the Father of the Western Monks

KING DAVID AND HIS SONGS
A Story of the Psalms

SAINT MARGARET MARY
And the Promises of the Sacred Heart of Jesus

SAINT JOHN MASIAS
Marvelous Dominican Gatekeeper of Lima, Peru

SAINT FRANCIS SOLANO
Wonder-Worker of the New World and Apostle of Argentina and Peru

BLESSED MARIE OF NEW FRANCE
The Story of the First Missionary Sisters in Canada

SAINT DOMINIC

PREACHER OF THE ROSARY AND
FOUNDER OF THE DOMINICAN ORDER

By
Mary Fabyan Windeatt

Illustrated by
Gedge Harmon

TAN BOOKS AND PUBLISHERS, INC.
Rockford, Illinois 61105

Nihil Obstat: Fintan G. Walker, Ph.D.
                   Censor Librorum

Imprimatur: ✠ Paul C. Schulte, D.D.
                   Archbishop of Indianapolis
                   July 13, 1948

This story of St. Dominic first appeared in serial form in the pages of *The Torch*. Published by Sheed & Ward in 1951 as simply *Saint Dominic*.

ISBN: 0-89555-430-5

Library of Congress Catalog Card No.: 93-61379

Printed and bound in the United States of America.

TAN BOOKS AND PUBLISHERS, INC.
P.O. Box 424
Rockford, Illinois 61105
1993

For
My Brothers and Sisters in the
Secular Third Order of Saint Dominic.

CONTENTS

O LIGHT of the Church, Doctor of Truth, rose of patience, ivory of chastity, freely hast thou dispensed the water of wisdom; Preacher of grace, unite us to the blessed.

—Feast of St. Dominic
Second Vespers,
Magnificat Antiphon

SAINT DOMINIC

CHAPTER 1

THE EARLY YEARS

IT WAS AUTUMN of the year 1190, and a blistering heat hung low over northern Spain like a breath from Hell. Throughout the kingdoms of Castile and Leon the crops failed. Burgos, Palencia, Valladolid—these and other cities were in the grip of the worst famine in years. People were dropping in the streets like flies, and there was rumor that soon the plague would strike.

"Mother of God, have pity on us!" was the anguished cry that went up from every heart. "Send us bread..."

But there was bread only for those who had money to buy it, and day after day the funeral bells sent out an almost constant dirge as mounds of sun-baked clay were heaped upon the bodies of still more victims of the famine. In Palencia things were especially serious, and finally one young man knew that he could stand it no longer. He, twenty-year-old Dominic de Guzman, a student for the priesthood, must do something to help the starving.

"But what *can* you do?" asked friends and

teachers anxiously. "Why, you are little more than a boy. . ."

"I know," admitted Dominic. "But I have some money. It will help to buy bread for at least one family."

Undaunted by the argument that he might as well keep what he had, since it was so little, Dominic went down into the poor section of Palencia and gave away all that he owned—his money, clothes, furniture from his room at school, and finally his books. It was a real sacrifice to part with the books, for they were sheets of precious parchment, that is, dried sheepskin, and of more than ordinary worth because of the many notes which were written in the margins.

"The lad must be a fool!" Dominic's friends told one another. "How can he keep at his studies without books?"

"That's right. How can he?"

But Dominic only smiled when such remarks reached his ears. "Who could prize dead skins when the flesh of the living is perishing from want?" he asked. "I'll manage somehow."

His faith was rewarded. After his great act of charity, Dominic enjoyed even more success at school than before—leading his classes in every subject, and making a name for himself as a scholar. Indeed, when the Bishop of Osma (a town near Palencia) heard about Dominic's fine record, and also how he had sold his precious books in order to help the poor, he made up his mind to one thing. Some day this courageous young man must come to live with him. As a priest he would make a fine assistant.

After his ordination in 1195, Dominic did go to Osma. And two years later when the Bishop died and Father Diego de Acebes succeeded to his position, nothing would do but that Dominic remain. He would be of great use as prior of the canons— that is, in charge of the assistant priests who lived in the Bishop's house.

Dominic was very happy at Osma. He liked the quiet life there, the chance to pray and study and to help out from time to time in the country parishes. Even more, he appreciated his friendship with Bishop Diego. What a saint this was! What a lover of souls!

"If the Holy Father ever permits him to be a missionary to the Tartars, I want to go along, too," Dominic told himself. "It would be a privilege to live and work with such a man for the rest of my days."

But the years passed, and Bishop Diego was unsuccessful in all his attempts to be relieved of his duties in Osma. He was needed there, said the authorities. And friends and co-workers agreed. Reluctantly he stifled his heart's desire to convert the Tartars—those savage tribes which lived along the Dnieper and Volga rivers in eastern Europe, and from time to time descended upon the Christian countries to the west with fire and sword.

"Lord, not my will but Thine be done!" he prayed.

Then one day there was great excitement in Osma. Bishop Diego was going away, although not to the Tartars. He was going to Denmark on important business for King Alfonso of Castile.

"It has something to do with a marriage for Prince Ferdinand," people said.

"That's right. King Alfonso has asked King Valdemar to let one of his daughters marry his son."

"Yes. And he wants Bishop Diego to help bring matters about."

So one morning in the year 1203, with Dominic as a traveling companion, the Bishop took his place among the dozens of learned priests and wealthy nobles who had been chosen by Alfonso as his ambassadors to the Danish court. But the imposing cavalcade had gone less than three hundred miles—indeed, had barely entered southern France —when scenes of great devastation met their eyes. Acres of fertile land lay blackened and desolate. Wayside shrines were broken. And one village after another lay in smoking ruins.

"What is it?" asked Dominic anxiously. "What's happened here?"

The questions were soon answered by a little group of peasants who timidly approached the royal procession to beg for food. The heretics— commonly known as the Albigenses because their teachings had originated in the French town of Albi—had caused all the damage, they said. Two days ago a band of them had come this way. Finding a few men and women faithful to the teachings of the Catholic Church, they had killed most of them, burned and pillaged their lands, then taken the children prisoner.

DOMINIC WAS BUSY DOLING OUT ALMS.

"Three of those little ones were my own grand-sons!" an old man told Diego, tears streaming down his withered cheeks. "Oh, Your Lordship! Isn't there anything that we can do?"

Diego looked at Dominic. "My son, you hear what this poor man says. What do you think?"

Dominic was busy doling out alms to the peasants. "We could drop out of line a while, Your Lordship," he suggested. "When these poor fellows have eaten, they'll be able to tell us more about what has happened, and perhaps we can figure out some way to help."

So Diego and Dominic left their places in the royal procession to attend to the peasants' wants and to hear what they had to say. Of course as priests they knew about the heresy of the Albigenses which had been afflicting southern France for several years. In fact, they were as much aware of its evils as they were of those existing in eastern Europe because of the pagan Tartars. Yet now the truth of the situation was fully brought home to them.

"Tell us about the heretics," said Bishop Diego presently. "Why do they act as they do?"

Refreshed with food and drink and heartened by the friendliness of Diego and Dominic, the peasants were soon vying with one another in explaining about the Albigenses—what they believed, and the cruelties which they practiced toward faithful mem-bers of the Catholic Church.

"The heretics claim that there are two gods, Your Lordship—one good and one bad."

"Yes. The good god made the soul, the bad god made the body."

"That's right. And since anything the bad god made is bad, it must be destroyed."

"So they practice suicide."

"And they don't believe in marriage."

"Or any of the Sacraments."

"They actually despise the Mass."

"And the Old Testament."

"And because we don't agree to their teachings, they burn our farms and destroy our churches."

Sorrow clouded the Bishop's face. "What do they do with the things which they take from the holy places?"

"Why, they keep them for their own use, Your Lordship."

"Even the sacred vessels?"

"Of course."

"But that's a sacrilege!"

"Yes, Your Lordship."

Soon further details were forthcoming. For instance, one reason that the heretics were so successful in southern France was their crafty leaders—men who seemed to have the cleverness of the devil himself. The powerful Count Raymond of Toulouse and Count Roger of Beziers had fallen so completely under the spell of these men as to give name and fortune to the cause.

"We do need help, Your Lordship!" cried the old man who had lost his grandsons. "One of these days the heretics will be back again. Then what's going to happen?"

But even as Diego groped for words to encourage him, there was a sound of galloping horses and two soldiers rode up breathlessly.

"Your Lordship, we've been waiting for you for over two hours! Is anything wrong?"

Diego pointed to the little group of peasants. "Father Dominic and I have been trying to help these poor people," he said. "They've told us how the heretics robbed them of everything—food, homes, children..."

The soldiers looked briefly at the peasants, then shook their heads grimly. "There are thousands more just like them. And there isn't anything anyone can do. The heretics are too powerful."

"But surely if we think about the problem..."

"There isn't time, Your Lordship. We have to be on our way."

With sinking heart the Bishop acknowledged that this was true. It was nearly a thousand miles to Denmark, and urgent work awaited everyone in the royal procession.

"My children," he sighed, turning to the peasants, "The best help I can give you at this time is prayer." Then, lifting his right hand, he spoke holy and familiar words over the forlorn little group before him:

"May the blessing of Almighty God—Father, Son and Holy Ghost—descend upon you and remain with you forever..."

CHAPTER 2

THE WORK BEGINS

THE NEXT SUMMER, before arrangements could be completed for the marriage of young Ferdinand of Castile with the Danish princess, the bride-to-be died. This freed Bishop Diego of his responsibilities as Alfonso's ambassador, and that same year—1204—he decided to go to Rome. He would make another attempt to be relieved of his duties in Osma so that he might take up missionary work among the Tartars. And Dominic would go with him to see the Holy Father.

But when the two stood before Pope Innocent the Third, it was clear that His Holiness was not going to grant the Bishop's request. For six years— in fact, ever since he had ascended the papal throne—he had been trying to do something about the heresy in southern France. Now he was really worried.

"My son, your work lies in the West," he told the Bishop. "Return there at once. The salvation of thousands is in peril."

In vain Diego pleaded the need for missionaries

"I'LL TRY TO HELP THE MONKS,
YOUR HOLINESS."

to go among the Tartars, as well as his own desire for martyrdom. The Pope was firm. In France conditions for the Church were serious. A year or so ago a few monks from the Abbey of Citeaux had gone to preach among the heretics, but to date their efforts had met with small success.

"The Abbot and his assistants are deeply discouraged," said Pope Innocent. "You must try to help them."

Realizing that a small act performed through holy obedience is of far more value in the eyes of God than a great act performed without it, Diego set aside, once and for all, his long-cherished hope of going to the Tartars.

"Very well. I'll try to help the monks, Your Holiness," he said.

"And you, my son?" said the Pope, turning to Dominic with a smile of relief. "You will try, too?"

Dominic's eyes shone. "Yes, Your Holiness. If you wish it."

So a few weeks later Diego and Dominic left Rome and returned to France. At the Abbey of Citeaux they took part in the Holy Week ceremonies. Then they set out for the city of Montpellier, where the Father Abbot and two monk helpers, Fathers Rudolph and Peter, were resting briefly from their labors among the heretics.

As they had expected, the newcomers found the missionaries very discouraged. They had preached hundreds of sermons, but to no avail. Long ago everyone in the countryside had been won over to the heresy of the Albigenses. Now the most eloquent words left them unmoved.

"If it weren't that the Holy Father himself had ordered us to try to convert these people, we'd return today to Citeaux," said the Abbot wearily. "Such a heartbreaking task as this we've never seen!"

Diego and Dominic agreed that the monks had good reason to feel discouraged. After all, hadn't Saint Bernard, the great light of their Order, been likewise disheartened more than fifty years before? Well, times had not changed. The heretics were still backed by ruthless and powerful men. It would take nothing short of a miracle to dislodge them and bring back southern France to the Catholic Faith.

"Since we're just beginning our work here, perhaps we'll be able to see the whole situation in a new light," Diego informed the Abbot. "That sometimes happens, you know. One or two changes in method could mean the difference between success and failure!"

"You're welcome to make all the changes you wish," said the Abbot. "Personally, though, I think that we've tried everything."

Some days later, however, when Diego offered his first suggestions—that in the future they should dress as poor men whenever they went out to preach among the heretics, that they should go barefoot and eat and lodge with peasants instead of at comfortable inns—the Abbot looked uneasy.

"That wouldn't be dignified," he objected.

Diego shrugged his shoulders. "Do we want dignity or do we want souls?"

"You don't understand. Here in France we monks represent His Holiness, Pope Innocent the Third. We are his ambassadors. To go about like beggars..."

Diego appeared not to hear. "We have another suggestion, too," he said. "My son," turning to Dominic, "will you explain what it is?"

Dominic smiled, knowing full well how his next words would affect the worthy Abbot of Citeaux.

"Father Abbot, we need women helpers," he said.

The Abbot stared. "*Women helpers?*"

"Yes, Father Abbot."

"But...but that's impossible! This preaching work we do is men's work—priestly work."

Dominic's face became grave. "Women helpers will mean the difference between success and failure," he declared. "Oh, Father Abbot! We must ask God to send us many of them! And right away!"

CHAPTER 3

A SIGN FROM HEAVEN

IT TOOK SOME TIME for the Abbot and his monks to come to Dominic's way of thinking, but in the end they were convinced. The heretics had many schools, most of which were in the charge of women. Here boys and girls were taught to hate the Sacraments, the Pope and much of the doctrine contained in the Creed. But if the Catholics could have schools, too...if there could be places where the children could learn the truth about God and His Church...

"It *would* make our work much easier," agreed the Abbot.

"Yes, and it would give women converts a safe place to stay," put in Father Rudolph. "I've heard that after their conversion they sometimes have to endure persecution from friends and relatives."

Father Peter agreed. "I've often asked myself how they ever dare to leave the heretics," he said. "But if we had schools...places of refuge, so to speak..."

However, the weeks passed, and there seemed

little hope of establishing the schools. Diego, Dominic and their co-workers had all they could do to move about from one place to another, preaching and instructing in the towns.

"Don't worry," said Bishop Foulques of Toulouse one day when the outlook seemed especially gloomy. "God is surely pleased with your efforts, and soon things will start to improve. In the meantime, I have some good news."

The missionaries looked at him eagerly. Bishop Foulques was their most important helper in the work they had come to do. Time and again he had encouraged them, and recently he had even come to their assistance by giving Dominic a small chapel in Fanjeaux.* Thus the little band of preachers now had a modest headquarters to which they could retire to pray and to make plans.

"And what would the good news be, Your Lordship?" asked Diego.

Bishop Foulques smiled. "Several of the most holy and learned priests in my diocese want to join you in your work."

There was a gasp of astonishment. Several learned and holy priests wanted to be missionaries among the Albigenses? How wonderful!

But almost at once a doubtful look crept into the eyes of the Abbot of Citeaux. "Do they know about the difficulties in the work?" he asked.

"Oh, yes," Bishop Foulques assured him. "And they are all eager to come."

---

*Pronunciation: Fa(n)-zhō (zh like s in the word measure).

Despite the arrival of the new helpers, Dominic frequently found himself discouraged, particularly as the spring days of the year 1206 rolled by. After twelve months in the field, how little had been accomplished! To make matters worse, sooner or later Bishop Diego would have to go back to Spain. And already he had insisted that, since the Abbot and his monks eventually would be returning to Citeaux, Dominic should take complete charge of the missionary work among the Albigenses. He was a good speaker. In fact, he was the best speaker in the group. No one was better suited than he for the post of superior.

Of course Dominic did not agree with Bishop Diego. He was just thirty-six years old, and most of his priestly life had been spent as the Bishop's assistant in the quiet little town of Osma. He knew far more about books that he did about preaching. Yet Diego was his superior and must be obeyed.

"I'll try to look after the work," he promised the Bishop. "I'll try very hard."

But, as time went on, Dominic's heart grew really heavy. Despite the prayers and sacrifices which he and his co-workers were offering for the Albigenses, they refused to be converted. It was easy and fashionable to be a heretic. There were no Commandments to keep, no particular moral duties for young or old.

"Certainly the devil has a stranglehold on these poor people," thought Dominic. "Dear Blessed Mother! Can't you help us to change all this?"

Then quite suddenly an extraordinary thing happened. The conviction grew in Dominic's soul that the Albigenses *would* be converted, and by none other than the Mother of God herself. The main thing necessary was that he and his preachers should be faithful to her in prayer, particularly in the prayer of the Hail Mary.

"The Hail Mary!" Dominic told himself eagerly. "We must start to say it as never before!"

Then presently Our Lady made known to Dominic a new way of praying Hail Marys.

Soon Dominic and the missionaries were stressing this new devotion. It consisted of one hundred and fifty Hail Marys to the Blessed Mother, divided into tens by Our Fathers—plus special considerations on the Mysteries of our Redemption—for the conversion of the Albigenses. The prayer, to be called the Rosary, borrowed its number from the number of Psalms in the Old Testament. But how much easier it was to say than those ancient prayers! And how much shorter! Why, the Hail Marys could be said while a person was walking to and from his work, or by peasants and little children who did not know how to read!

"Your Lordship, we're going to win our fight against the heretics by the power of the Hail Mary and the Rosary," Dominic declared.

"You're right," Bishop Diego agreed. "Our Lady *will* help us to win out over the Evil One."

Meanwhile Bishop Diego and his co-workers moved tirelessly about the French countryside. They wore plain tunics of white wool covered by linen surplices and black wool mantles—in fact, the garb which was worn by the assistant priests in Diego's cathedral in Osma. Yet how different their work! Of course they still praised God each day in the Psalms and other prayers of the Divine Office, but now there was an extensive preaching program as well. Sometimes they spoke in the marketplace, debating with the heretics on this or that point of doctrine. At others, they spoke in private homes, in castles, in churches—wherever a crowd could be gathered.

"But it's not enough," Dominic admitted to himself. "People are dying in error even as we preach. Oh, Blessed Mother! Surely there must be something else that we can do? Surely you have some kind of plan for us, to hasten the work and to make it fruitful?"

On July 22, 1206, Feast of Saint Mary Magdalen, Dominic was in Fanjeaux, where Bishop Foulques had given him the chapel which provided a headquarters for the missionaries. It had been a very hot day, and as evening came on Dominic decided to take a walk. His steps led him toward the north gates of the town, where there was a splendid view of the surrounding countryside, of valley and hill and forest, touched now by the rich colors of the setting sun. In the distance rose the stone citadel of Carcassonne, shining like a palace of gold. Nearer was Montreal, with its towers and walls and rooftops of glittering tile.

Dominic looked about him. "How beautiful it all is!" he thought, gazing out upon the vast panorama before him. Then slowly his eyes clouded. Yes, the

A GLOBE OF WHITE FLAME APPEARED
IN THE TWILIGHT.

scene was a beautiful one. But what a pity that
heresy had made such progress here! In castle and
fortress, in the homes of noble and peasant, the
destructive doctrines of the Albigenses were being
fostered as nowhere else in France. At this very
moment hundreds of little children were being
taught to hate the Mass, the Sacraments, the very
Word of God!

"And it's the mothers and the aunts and the
grandmothers who are largely responsible,"
Dominic told himself. "The devil is making use of
their ignorance to keep the next generation from
knowing and loving the Heavenly Father."

Presently the sunset faded and shadows closed
in upon the valley below Fanjeaux. Yet the solitary
man standing outside the north gates of the town
scarcely noticed the change. If only something
could be done to drive heresy from the hearts of
the women in southern France! Then surely half
the battle would be won, for the children would
be saved. And the men—well, eventually they
would follow where the women and children led.

"Schools," murmured Dominic, "convents of
women devoted to God's service. . ."

Suddenly an extraordinary thing happened. Out
of the deep twilight appeared a globe of white
flame. For a moment the strange light hovered
unsteadily in the sky; then it brightened, and with
a trail of glory moved across the heavens and came
to rest above a church in the valley.

Dominic stared. He could see that the white
light was hovering above the roof of Saint Mary of

Prouille,* a forlorn little chapel below Fanjeaux where only a few people ever came to pray!

"What does it mean?" he whispered, carried out of himself with awe. Then a mysterious voice spoke within his heart:

"My son, you have asked me for help. Behold the little church at Prouille. Here you will begin your life's real work. Here you will save many souls for Heaven."

With a thrill of pure joy Dominic realized it was the Blessed Mother who was speaking to him. But as a host of questions rose to his lips, the radiance bathing the little church in the valley below faded into the shadows. And the voice spoke no more. He was alone in the darkness of his lofty vantage point outside the north gates of Fanjeaux.

Fearful that the marvel he had witnessed might have been a dream, Dominic came the next evening to the same place—prayerful and eager. Was the Blessed Mother pleased with him and with the Hail Marys which he and his followers were offering to her each day? Did she really have a plan for converting the Albigenses in which the little church in the valley would play a part?

As twilight fell, the wonders of the previous night were repeated. A globe of white flame appeared, hovered for a moment over the valley, then came to rest above the deserted Church of Saint Mary. And the same words echoed in Dominic's heart: *"My son, you have asked me for help. Behold the*

*Pronunciation: Proo ee′

*little church at Prouille. Here you will begin your
life's real work. Here you will save many souls for
Heaven."*

When the marvel was repeated for a third time
on the following night, Dominic hesitated no
longer. The globe of light and the voice in his heart
were not the products of his imagination. They
were real.

"I agree with you, my son," said Bishop Diego
when he had heard about the wonder. "The
Blessed Mother certainly has work for us to do at
Prouille. But what?"

"I don't know, Your Lordship."

"It can't be preaching. The place is too far off
the beaten path for anyone to come to listen to us."

Dominic's eyes clouded. How truly the Bishop
spoke! And yet. . .

"Perhaps at Prouille we are to have a house for
our women converts," he said. "Your Lordship, how
wonderful that would be!"

The Bishop hesitated. "Perhaps. But as yet our
women converts can be counted on the fingers of
one hand. And they are hardly the kind who are
free or suited to lead the religious life."

For a time Dominic was silent. Then he lifted
his eyes to those of the Bishop. "We've had one sign
from Heaven," he said. "I'm sure that there's going
to be another."

"Another?"

"Yes, Your Lordship. And what great rejoicing
this one will bring with it when it comes!"

CHAPTER 4

LIFE AT PROUILLE

WITHIN A FEW WEEKS Dominic had occasion to address nine women heretics in his little chapel at Fanjeaux.

"My daughters, what a pity that you insist on remaining in the devil's power!" he said. "How can you ever hope to be happy?"

At once cries of protest arose from the group. In the power of the devil? What a falsehood! Why, they were all women of noble birth and good education! Their families were among the richest and most prominent in the whole countryside. Even Count Raymond of Toulouse and Count Roger of Beziers, those powerful men among the Albigenses, were pleased to call them friends.

"It's you who are in the devil's power, Father," declared a young girl named Gentiana, "you and all these other wandering priests who've been preaching in our towns."

"That's right!" cried a woman whose name was Claretta. "And your Bishop Diego—he's nothing but a hypocrite! I've watched him closely, and I know."

23

"He thinks he can come here and tell us what to do!"

"Let him go back to Spain where he belongs!"

"Let the Abbot of Citeaux go home, too!"

"And his monks!"

"Yes! We've had enough of meddlers!"

Dominic paid no attention to the outburst. "You *are* in the devil's power, my poor children," he repeated. "You don't know what you are saying."

Then he went on to speak of the Heavenly Father and the Church which His Son had founded upon earth some twelve hundred years before. Of course this Church was the true one, and its teachings the only ones which would lead a person to eternal happiness in Heaven.

"How could the one true Church teach untruth?" he asked, his eyes ranging eagerly from one hostile face to the next. "How can it be possible that the Sacraments are evil if they were instituted by God Himself, who is all good?"

"Don't forget that there are two gods, Father— one good and the other bad," jibed a third speaker. "Every child knows that!"

For a moment Dominic was silenced, his eyes full of compassion. What ignorance was here! What stubborn prejudice! Yet the Blessed Virgin knew all this far better than he.

"Dearest Mother, help me to enlighten them!" he begged. "Even though they *are* heretics, they are still your children."

Presently he began to speak again. In simple words he pointed out that even a small lie has power to sadden and destroy. Then what about big lies? Lies which concern God and His Commandments? The destiny of entire nations?

"The devil is the father of the first and worst of lies," he declared. "He lied to Eve in the Garden of Eden. He made her doubt and then disbelieve what God had told her. He promised her great power and happiness if only she would eat of the forbidden fruit. But did she find this power and happiness? Did she find anything but pain, sorrow, exile. . ."

Suddenly a scream tore through the chapel. "Oh, Father! Look!"

At once all eyes turned to a woman named Curtolana. Pale as death, she was pointing a trembling finger at something creeping in the aisle. They all looked, and what a loathsome sight met their eyes! It was an animal, shaped like a huge black cat. But it was no cat! Its eyes were those of an ox—its dripping red tongue at least six inches in length, its tail long and bushy like that of a dog. And as it moved stealthily forward, sniffing and growling, its glittering eyes rolled from side to side as though in search of a victim.

Fear seized every heart. What manner of creature was this? Where had it come from? What was it going to do?

"Don't let it touch me, Father!" screamed Claretta.

"No! No!" cried Gentiana.

Then all the women were screaming together.

Dominic paid slight heed to the terrified women,

IT CLUNG FOR AN INSTANT TO THE BELLROPE.

for his eyes were fixed upon the fearsome beast advancing closer and closer. Suddenly his face grew stern and he raised his hand threateningly. "Begone, Satan!" he ordered. "In the Name of the one true God!"

Its eyes flashing fire, the animal stopped in its tracks. Then, with a snarl of rage, it leaped over the heads of the women, clung for an instant to a bellrope that was hanging near the wall, and vanished into the ceiling in a cloud of evil-smelling smoke.

For an instant there was a stunned silence. Then, without exception, the women burst into tears.

"Oh, Father! You...you saved our lives!"

"It was just about to spring, Father, when you spoke!"

"A few seconds more and it would have clawed out our eyes!"

Pale, but with firm tread, Dominic came down the aisle to comfort his congregation. "Don't be afraid, my children," he said gently. "The wretched beast is gone now."

Gentiana clasped her hands. "But what was it, Father?" she wailed, sending a quick and fearful glance at the ceiling.

Dominic hesitated. "It was the devil in one of his evil forms," he said. Then he began to speak again of God, of His Church, of the dreadful heresy of the Albigenses which was designed to tear this Church apart even as the dreadful beast had wanted to rend their human bodies.

As he spoke, Dominic watched their faces, and

how changed they were! Just a few minutes before,
each woman had been ready to argue, even to ridi-
cule. Now they listened eagerly to every word.

"Oh, Father! We believe everything that you
say!" they cried. "We've been wrong! Terribly
wrong! What must we do to make up for our
error?"

Dominic's heart sang as he surveyed the group
before him. Nine converts, and at once! Never in
his three years of preaching had he known such
success. Yet, when he spoke, his voice was calm.

"You must come to Confession," he said, "then
publicly renounce the teachings of the heretics.
After that..."

"Yes?" put in Gentiana quickly. "Then what must
we do, Father?"

Dominic smiled. "I think that the Blessed
Mother will be the one to answer that question,"
he said. "We must ask her help to discover God's
Will for you."

After several weeks of prayer and thought,
Dominic was satisfied that he had received Our
Lady's answer. The nine converts had not had an
easy time of it at home since their conversion. It
would be best if they could find other living
quarters.

"At Prouille," Dominic told Diego. "Oh, Your
Lordship, I'm sure that the Blessed Mother wishes
to have the nine women established there!"

"In a convent?"

"Yes, Your Lordship—attached to the little
chapel. Then they can pray for the success of our

work and care for other women converts whom we may send them. Perhaps they could care for a few children, and thus save them from heresy!"

Diego's eyes were thoughtful. "That *is* an idea," he said. "After all, an active work such as preaching is of little use without prayer and good works behind it."

Dominic's nine converts were more than willing to form themselves into a religious community, and arrangements were made with Bishop Foulques of Toulouse that the Church of Saint Mary at Prouille, together with the surrounding grounds, should be given into their care. By November 22, four months after Dominic had seen the mysterious globe of white flame hovering over the deserted property, a small house had been made ready. And on December 27 the nine women came there to begin the religious life.

The rule which Dominic gave his new community placed great emphasis on prayer and penance. While he and Bishop Diego and their helpers preached the True Faith about the countryside, the Sisters at Prouille were expected to win for them the necessary graces. Several times a day they were to join together, even as the preachers, in offering the official prayer of the Church—the Divine Office. They were not to leave their convent home, but were to maintain a strict cloister. Except during brief periods of recreation, there was to be silence at all times. And although all nine were members of noble families and possessed of a good education, they were not to shun the tasks of the poor, such as spinning and weaving. Even more. Several days in the week were to be observed as fast days. Only a little food was to be taken, and various other sacrifices were to be offered to God.

"Tell me—is this new life too hard?" Dominic asked one day, rather anxiously.

Gentiana's eyes were full of peace. "Oh, Father, I don't think any sacrifice is too hard when I remember it can save souls for Heaven," she declared.

Her sisters in religion—Curtolana, Claretta, Berengaria, Raymunda, Adelaide, Jordana, Wilhelmina and Richarde—heartily agreed. Despite the opposition of friends and relatives, they were supremely happy at Prouille. What a joy to wear the linen veil and plain white woolen habit which Father Dominic had given them! What a privilege to play a part with him in converting France from heresy!

"We are helping you, aren't we, Father?" they would ask. "We are making up for our sins and the sins of others by this new life?"

Dominic always reassured them. "Only after death," he said, "will you know how much!"

During the next few months life at Prouille went on in orderly and tranquil fashion, disturbed by only one incident. Bishop Diego announced that he was returning to Osma. He had been absent from his diocese for more than two years, and important matters there were claiming his attention.

Distressed as Dominic and his spiritual daughters were over the departure of their good friend

and superior, they had much for which to be thank-
ful. For instance, there were now fairly numerous
conversions resulting from the sermons given by
Dominic and his assistants in town and village.
Then again, Prouille itself was beginning to grow.
Recently two girls from Fanjeaux had been admitted as novices, while seven or eight children had
been brought to the convent by their parents to
receive Christian training. Through the influence
of Bishop Foulques of Toulouse, gifts of land and
money had been received. Now a new building was
rising close to the Church of Saint Mary. God willing, in a few months it would serve as a permanent
headquarters for Dominic and his preachers.

"I'm sure that all of this has come through our
devotion to the Blessed Mother," Dominic declared.
"If only the whole world could know the power for
good that lies in the prayer which she loves so
much—the Rosary!"

The Sisters at Prouille and the priests who were
his helpers shared Dominic's opinion. A Hail Mary
took only a few seconds to say. Even one hundred
and fifty Hail Marys—Our Lady's Psalter, or the
complete Rosary—could be offered in a comparatively short time. "Some day," they said, "the whole
world will know the power of this prayer!"

But the community was not to live in peace for
long. One day in the year 1208 a shocking report
reached Prouille. Father Peter (the monk who had
been one of the first to work among the Albigenses)
had been found cruelly murdered by the heretics,
and word was going about that other priests who

persisted in upholding the teachings of the Church of Rome would meet with a like fate.

"We've had enough of you meddling preachers," was the message which came from the headquarters of the heretics. "Get out of southern France at once!"

CHAPTER 5

THE WAR YEARS

A S EVERYONE KNEW, the murder of Father Peter had been ordered by Count Raymond of Toulouse because the monk had first dared to reprove him for his excesses; then, as ambassador from the Holy See, to excommunicate him.

"This slaying of a holy priest is no ordinary crime," Bishop Foulques told Dominic. "Everyone knows that to murder an ambassador is an outrage. But to murder an ambassador from the Holy Father. . ."

Dominic's eyes flashed. "Raymond has offered a challenge, not only to us in France but to the whole Christian world!" he declared. "Oh, Your Lordship! Surely the Holy Father can be patient no longer! Surely he must act at once—*and with force!*"

Dominic was right. Already time had shown there was not the slightest chance that Count Raymond would repent his evil deed. This was but the climax of a series of crimes which he had committed against the Church. Over and over again priests and Bishops had begged him to be merciful when his plundering armies swept through the countryside—not to be so greedy for power, to spare the poor and innocent, the churches and monasteries. But he had never deigned to listen. The son of an Albigensian mother, he had been wild and headstrong since boyhood, refusing to recognize any authority, even that of God. Now he had issued the supreme challenge. Who was greater—Raymond of Toulouse, or Pope Innocent the Third?

Within a few months' time thousands of Christian men had rallied to Pope Innocent's cause, not only in France but in Germany, England and Spain. Accompanied by their priests and Bishops, they came to do battle for the Church. And not unwillingly, either. They were convinced that there was no other way for truth and justice to triumph than by force of arms.

Dominic witnessed the new turn of events with mixed feelings. Of course the war declared against Count Raymond was a holy war. And yet what sorrow it would bring! What hardship for everyone involved! However, his spirits lifted somewhat when word came of the appointment of an English noble, Count Simon de Montfort, as leader of the Catholic armies. The latter was a brave Christian soldier, long experienced in warfare, whose very name was sufficient to strike terror into cowardly hearts.

"Already some of the heretics have begged for peace," announced Brother Bertrand, one of Dominic's assistants. "Oh, if only the war would last just a short time, and Count Raymond would consent to mend his ways!"

But soon it became evident that this was not to be. The English leader, able general though he was, had to labor under tremendous handicaps. For instance, he employed no hordes of ruthless brigands, such as served Count Raymond of Toulouse. Rather, his armies were composed largely of peasants, or of men who were less interested in fighting than in gaining the indulgences attached to defending the Catholic cause. Since only a few weeks' military service was required to gain these indulgences, Simon's followers would sometimes number into the thousands, only to be reduced to a handful of men a few weeks later—the former soldiers having returned to their homes, feeling that their duty was done!

"This war is going to be a long one after all," Dominic acknowledged. "Oh, dear Blessed Mother! What are we going to do?"

Somehow there seemed to be no answer to his prayer, but Dominic did not give up hope. A friendship gradually sprang up between himself and Count Simon de Montfort, and frequently the two spent some days in each other's company. In fact, much against his wishes, Dominic found himself forced to take an active part in the conflict against the Albigenses. Of course he did not go into battle, but since he was a learned priest, not restricted to serving God in a monastery, he was prevailed upon to travel with Simon's armies and act as a judge for the heretics who were made prisoner. Another of his duties was to restore Catholic worship in the captured towns. Then again, he did great good in maintaining Christian principles among Simon's own men.

Dominic's presence was a great consolation to the English general. "Please don't ever think of leaving us, Father!" he often begged. "We need you so much..."

For several years Dominic gave in to Simon's wishes, remaining in France and doing his best to convert the captured heretics through prayer and preaching. By now his reputation as a kind and just judge was solidly established, and gradually many of his former enemies became friends. However, there were still some who did not believe the good things said of him and thirsted for a chance to do him harm. Dominic knew this but was undisturbed. To be a martyr for the Catholic Faith would mean that one would go straight to Heaven!

"I think I know a good way to become a martyr," he told himself one day. "I'll go to Carcassonne alone!"

The small town of Carcassonne was a hotbed of heresy. Catholics there suffered all manner of persecution—from being pelted with mud and stones to outright torture and death. But Dominic entered its gates light-heartedly, singing a favorite hymn to the Blessed Mother—*Alma Redemptoris Mater*—as he walked along.

First the heretics were startled, then furious. "What's Father Dominic doing in Carcassonne?" they wanted to know. "Isn't he supposed to be with

de Montfort's men? And why is he singing? Doesn't
he realize what's in store for him here?"

Presently Dominic himself had answered all
these questions. Lately the war had been going well
for the Catholic armies. He could be spared for a
time, especially as one of his assistants had taken
his place at de Montfort's headquarters. As for singing Our Lady's hymn—well, why shouldn't he? He
was happy, and to sing the lovely hymn made him
happier still.

"After all, I understand that you plan to kill me,"
he said, smiling. "Ah, my friends, how good to know
that I'll soon be in Heaven!"

The heretics stared. What manner of man was
this black-and-white-clad preacher to dare to call
them friends? Not to be a bit afraid of them?

"He's a fool!" muttered an ugly-faced youth. "But
wait until night comes. He'll sing a different tune
when we show our knives and daggers."

"Burning at the stake would be better," whispered a companion. "Ah, to see him begging for
mercy as his flesh roasts!"

"That's right," growled a third. "But first we'll
have some sport with him."

"We'll put out his eyes!"

"We'll cut off his fingers!"

"Yes, and slowly—one at a time!"

Dominic laughed as the whispered threats grew
louder. But far from cringing before his enemies,
he strolled carefree through the town. Up one
street and down the next he went, singing still more
hymns in his fine, clear voice. Occasionally he even

"LET THE FOOL BE!"

stopped to preach to his tormentors and to bless children who stared at him from doorways in round-eyed wonder. But the climax came when night fell. Then he spread his cloak upon the village green, offered a few prayers, and lay down to rest in full view of his enemies.

The heretics could scarcely believe their eyes. Fuming and cursing, they circled about the quiet figure, fingering their knives and daggers. Here certainly was the chance for which they had been waiting. But now that it was here, what good was it? There was little sport in attacking a man who laughed at danger, who had even thanked them in advance for their kindness in killing him. Why, Father Dominic had gone so far as to agree that it would be best to use the slowest and most painful methods possible in putting him to death!

"In that way I'll have much more merit," he had explained pleasantly.

For several minutes the heretics milled about in the darkness, confused and disappointed. "Well, what do we do—kill him or not?" asked one man irritably. "We can't stay here all night."

There was a renewed consultation, punctuated with much noise and argument. What was the use of killing a man who placed such little value on his life? Then the leader of the heretics spat in disgust. "Let the fool be!" he sneered. "We'll find some other priest who'll make much better sport."

The next morning Dominic arose early, spent a few minutes in prayer, then once more began a tour of Carcassonne—giving notice to all that he was still on hand by his loud and cheerful singing. By this time the heretics' anger had given way to a curiosity which they were scarcely able to disguise. From time to time some of them even found themselves lending an ear to his preaching as he went from one part of town to another.

"This priest does have a way with words," one man admitted grudgingly. "I don't think I ever heard anyone speak so well."

CHAPTER 6

ANOTHER TRIP TO ROME

THE WAR CONTINUED, with fair success for the Catholic cause. But by the year 1215, Dominic felt that he had spent enough time at the battlefront. It was now seven years since the heretics had murdered Father Peter, and the struggle between de Montfort and Count Raymond had turned into a complex affair, with the religious issue frequently clouded by the political.

"My son, I think that you've more than done your part in the war," Bishop Foulques decided one day. "Won't you consider coming with me to Rome? I'm planning to attend an important meeting there."

Dominic's heart beat fast at the thought. More than eleven years had passed since he had visited Rome. He had had comparatively little experience with people then, despite his thirty-four years. And the chief aim of his companion and superior, Bishop Diego, had been to secure the Holy Father's permission to go as a missionary to the Tartars. But how different now! He himself was a man of forty-five—widely-traveled, widely-experienced—and with a plan about which the Holy Father must hear sooner or later.

"Your Lordship, I'd like nothing better than to go with you to Rome," he declared.

In August of that same year, the Bishop and Dominic set out on their six-hundred-mile journey to Rome. They traveled on foot, arriving early in September for the opening of the meeting in which Bishop Foulques was so much interested—the Fourth Council of the Lateran.

Of course Dominic was interested in the Council, too, and planned to attend the meetings. But at the first opportunity he sought out the Holy Father privately and set before him the plan which had been the real reason for his coming to Rome. He wanted to found a religious order—one entirely different from any existing in the Church!

"It would be an Order of preachers and teachers," he explained. "Oh, Your Holiness! What a great need there is for such an order these days!"

Pope Innocent the Third looked up in joyful amazement. For years he had hoped for just such news as this. But where was the man to organize the work? Where was the scholar, the teacher, the preacher, *the saint,* to bring it into being?

"My son, tell me all about your plan!" he cried. "It sounds almost too good to be true."

So Dominic launched into an account of what he and his followers had done in southern France during the last eleven years. First, they had established a convent of cloistered nuns who prayed and made sacrifices to secure God's blessing upon the work of preaching. Second, they had converted several hundred heretics. Third, they were now known as Bishop Foulques' chief assistants—"The Preachers of the Diocese of Toulouse." But they wanted to be much more. They wanted to labor in all the great cities of Europe; to travel from place to place, preaching and teaching.

"And we want to do these things as real religious, Your Holiness—as members of an order consecrated to God," concluded Dominic.

"How would you support yourselves?" asked the Pope.

"We'd live on alms, Your Holiness."

For a moment the Pope said nothing. Then a smile of deep content crossed his face. "My son, this is the best news that I've heard in a long time," he declared. "When the Council opens, you must tell the delegates about your plan. Until then..."

"Yes, Your Holiness?"

"Pray to the Holy Spirit for enlightenment. The devil must never be allowed to hinder your wonderful work."

So Dominic set himself to praying as never before, one of his favorite retreats being the Basilica of Saint Peter. And one night while he knelt there, a glorious vision came to strengthen his faith. He saw the figure of Our Lord holding three arrows, with which He seemed ready to punish the world for its sins. Suddenly the Blessed Virgin appeared, prostrated before her Son, then presented two men—the first dressed in a rough grey habit with

IT WAS THE GREY-CLAD FIGURE OF HIS VISION!

a cord about his waist, the second garbed in a surplice and a tunic of white wool with a black mantle over it. These men, she indicated, had done no harm. In fact, they would convert many sinners and so appease the divine anger. Because of them, the world must be spared.

Dominic stared in amazement. *Could one of the men be himself? Yes, surely it was so! But who was the other, apparently in his early thirties, and with the happiest smile that he had ever seen?*

Slowly the vision faded, and Dominic was left to figure out it's meaning as best he could. But it was only the next day that everything was made clear. Then in the Basilica of Saint Peter he saw the grey-clad figure of his vision—*in person!* Quickly he arose from his knees to address him. "Who are you?" he gasped.

Smiling, the stranger stretched out both arms. "I? Why, I'm Brother Francis of Assisi," he said. "Welcome, Brother Dominic!"

Joyfully the two embraced, Dominic's heart all but bursting with happiness as Francis assured him that soon all would be well for the new Order of Preachers.

"Five years ago I came here to have my own work approved," he explained. "Then three years ago again. Don't be discouraged if there is some delay about details. Cast your cares upon the Lord, and He will sustain you."

As they left Saint Peter's together, Francis began to outline the work which he and his followers were trying to do in Italy. In one sense, it was similar

to Dominic's—preaching God's Word along the
highways and byways. Yet in another, it was vastly
different. Whereas Dominic and his assistants dis-
puted points of doctrine with the heretics, especially with their scholars and leaders, Francis and
his brethren, being laymen (that is, not priests), con-
tented themselves with preaching the Gospels. And
since so many great families in Italy had fallen away
from the Christian ideals because of the luxury in
their lives, Francis and his friars had given away all
personal goods. They owned nothing. Even their
food and clothing were begged from door to door.

"There's nothing like being poor for Christ's
sake!" cried Francis. "If a man has possessions, he
has to have weapons with which to defend them.
And from having property and weapons comes
strife with neighbors and relatives, so that charity
to God and to men suffers many a scar. Don't you
agree?"

Dominic did agree, and in the weeks that followed he listened eagerly to other things which
Francis had to say. Then one day came exciting
news from the Vatican—

"Last night I had a vision," Pope Innocent
informed Dominic. "It seemed that our great Basilica of Saint John Lateran was about to fall. Deep
cracks were in the walls. The roof was giving way.
Then you—"

"I, Your Holiness?"

"You appeared, put your shoulders to the walls,
and then...why, you grew to giant stature! You
stretched up your arms and supported the tottering

building without the least strain! In the space of an instant your mere touch had repaired all the damage. The church was as good as new."

As Dominic stood dumbfounded, Pope Innocent's voice took on even graver tones. "This isn't just the foolish dream of an old man, my son," he declared earnestly.

"Oh, no, Your Holiness. But still. . ."

"Listen. Some years ago I had a like vision. Only then it was our little friend from Assisi, Brother Francis who appeared to me. At that time he was here in Rome trying to obtain approval for the work of his begging friars. At first I was advised not to give it, for his ideas seemed too extreme for our times. But then came the vision, just like the one of last night, and I knew that Francis was right. If poverty were preached to the people—and I mean that poverty which is embraced for love of Christ—false standards would disappear. There would be a new spiritual freedom in Italy, even throughout the world."

Dominic listened in silence as Pope Innocent went on to say that his faith in Brother Francis had not been mistaken. Many souls had been saved through the work of his friars during the past few years. But his heart all but burst for joy when the Pope declared that he, Dominic, had also been raised up by God to do a special work for souls. Without delay the new preaching and teaching Order—the Order of Friars Preachers—must be gotten underway.

"Go back to France at once," urged the Pope.

"Call your brethren together, and decide upon a Rule. Then let me know your choice."

In just a few days Dominic was on his way. And with what joy! Even Bishop Foulques was amazed. Finally he felt called upon to issue a warning.

"There may be many delays before you and your followers can agree upon a Rule," he pointed out. "And have you thought of this: If you are to go in for preaching on a really great scale, what about vocations? With only six helpers. . ."

Dominic laughed at his good friend's serious manner. "All that matters just now is that the Holy Father is on our side," he insisted. "Oh, Your Lordship, how glad I am that I came to Rome!"

Sighing, the Bishop shook his head. Who could hope to dampen the enthusiasm of a man like Father Dominic—especially when the salvation of souls was at stake? But upon arriving in Toulouse, the Bishop soon found himself becoming excited about the future of the new Order of Preachers. During the absence, Dominic's helpers had increased from six to sixteen. Some were living at Prouille, others in Toulouse, in a house which had been given to Dominic some months ago by Peter Seila, a devout layman.

"Why, I can hardly believe it!" cried the Bishop. *"Sixteen helpers!"*

"Yes, Your Lordship," replied Dominic. "But we must remember that it's only a beginning. With God's help, many more generous-hearted men will come to join us."

Soon arrangements were made for the brethren

who were living in Peter Seila's house in Toulouse to go to Prouille. In this place, where ten years ago the Blessed Mother had indicated that Dominic's life work should begin, a religious Rule would be chosen by the new community.

It was no ordinary company that met at Prouille in mid-April of the year 1216. There were seven Frenchmen, six Spaniards, one Portuguese, one Belgian and one Englishman. Some were priests, some clerics not yet ordained, some laymen. But they were united by their deep faith in Dominic's ideals and their desire to give themselves to God's service in his community.

It did not take long to choose a Rule. After a period of fervent prayer, the sixteen voted to live according to the time-honored Rule of Saint Augustine. It was a way of life whereby thousands of men and women had attained sanctity. Moreover, it was a flexible Rule, and would lend itself easily to the special needs of preachers and teachers.

"Now we can start to serve God properly," announced Suero Gomez, the Portuguese member of the community. "Oh, Father! Every day you will explain parts of the Rule to us. And if we have any doubts or difficulties. . ."

Dominic shook his head. "Brother Bertrand will be explaining the Rule to you, not I. I'm returning to Rome."

Suero's eyes widened in astonishment. "But Father! You just came from there! Surely you're not thinking of going again?"

Quickly Brother Lawrence from England and

Brother Stephen from Belgium stepped forward
with a series of protests.

"It's six hundred miles to Rome, Father."

"Yes, and you just walked both ways."

"You need a rest after such a long, hard trip."

"You owe it to us to take better care of your
health."

Dominic laughed heartily. "Now, now! Don't
worry about my health. I'm strong and hardy.
Besides, I promised His Holiness that I would let
him know in person when we had decided upon
a Rule. Would you have me break my word?"

Reluctantly the sixteen agreed that another trip
to Rome was necessary. But of course Father
Dominic would not stay long? He would come back
to them as soon as possible?

"God willing, I'll be back in just a few months,"
Dominic promised.

CHAPTER 7

A YEAR IN TOULOUSE

BEFORE DOMINIC LEFT for Rome, Bishop Foulques made him a most valuable gift— the chapel of Saint Romanus in Toulouse— with the suggestion that a proper monastery be built on the grounds. After all, he said, the city of Toulouse was a far better center for the new Order than either Fanjeaux or Prouille. And now that Dominic's helpers numbered sixteen, Peter Seila's house was much too small.

Dominic agreed. "Saint Romanus will be our first real monastery," he said. "Oh, Your Lordship, how delighted Pope Innocent will be that you have made us this gift!"

But before work could be started on the new monastery, distressing news came from Rome. Pope Innocent was dead! To make matters worse, even after the monastery was finished and Dominic had arrived in Rome, it was impossible to see the new Pope—Honorius the Third. He was absent on important business, and no one seemed to know when he would return.

"GO AND PREACH,
FOR TO THIS WORK YOU ARE CALLED."

"Dear Lord, will he give our Order his blessing?" Dominic wondered anxiously. "Will he be as kind and understanding as Pope Innocent?"

The days passed, and there seemed to be no answer to these questions. Then one night when he was at prayer in the great Basilica of Saint Peter, peace came to Dominic's troubled heart. Once again he was granted a wonderful grace—a vision of Saints Peter and Paul, in which the former bestowed upon him a pilgrim's staff, the latter a book of the Gospels.

"Go and preach, for to this work you are called," the two Apostles said. Then, as this vision passed, there came a second one, in which Dominic saw his brethren going forth two by two throughout the whole world to preach the Word of God to white men, yellow men, black men—indeed, to every race under the sun.

It seemed a long time before Dominic came to himself and grasped the full meaning of the visions, but as the realization grew steadily clearer, he breathed an ardent prayer of thanksgiving. What matter now the many difficulties in establishing his religious family? *"Go and preach, for to this work you are called!"* Ah, there was no mistaking the import of these words!

"Pope Honorius *will* give us his blessing!" he told himself. "I know it!"

Dominic's faith was rewarded. Within a few days His Holiness returned to Rome, and before long the two had become close friends. Indeed, the new pontiff was so impressed by Dominic's sanctity and zeal, the clear explanation of his work and plans, that the long-sought approval for the Order of Preachers was wholeheartedly given. And not in just one official document, but in several.

"We," declared Honorius, "considering that the brethren of your Order will be the champions of the Faith and true light of the world, do confirm the Order in all its land and possessions, present and to come; and we take the Order itself, with all its goods and rights, under our protection and government."

Of course Dominic was delighted—not only that his work now had the blessing of the Holy See, but that he himself possessed a new and good friend in Pope Honorius. Yet as he made preparations for the homeward journey to Toulouse, he was hardly prepared for the honor suddenly bestowed upon him.

"My son, it would please me very much if you would postpone your trip for a while," said the Pope. "Could you...that is, would you...stay in Rome for a few more weeks?"

Dominic stared. "A few more weeks, Your Holiness?"

"Yes, I know you promised your brethren that you would return to them as soon as possible. But the people of our city have need of good preachers, too. Why not give them the chance to hear you speak?"

Dominic recognized the honor which the Pope was paying him by inviting him to prolong his visit, and so he gratefully accepted. By special arrangement of His Holiness, he preached each day in a different church. He met many interesting and important people, too, and had several visits with his good friend from Assisi, Brother Francis. In fact, as the days passed, he became really well known.

"Father Dominic is the best preacher I've ever heard," declared Cardinal Ugolino (who one day would guide the fortunes of the Church as Pope Gregory the Ninth). "They tell me the greatest sinners are being converted through his sermons."

"That's right," put in another Cardinal. "And have you noticed how the young people take to him? Believe me, if he stays with us much longer, our finest young men will be off to France to join his Order."

Back in Toulouse, however, there was a growing impatience at the delay in Father Dominic's return. What had happened, anyway? Why didn't Father Dominic come back to the new monastery of Saint Romanus as he had promised? Had Pope Honorius refused his blessing? Was it going to be necessary to break up the work? Then one day in May all these questions were answered. Dominic arrived with the documents of papal approval and with news of tremendous importance as well. Within three months the Order of Preachers would make a foundation in Paris! And in Madrid, too!

"You're going to branch out," declared Dominic triumphantly. "You're going to carry God's Word to hundreds and thousands of people in Europe!"

The sixteen brethren were overjoyed at the sight of their beloved Father and at the news that Pope

Honorius had finally established them as a religious order in the Church. But they were far from happy over the thought of leaving Toulouse. Not that they were averse to working for souls, of course. This was their vocation. But to be sent away so soon—to have to build monasteries, fill them with religious, preach and study and minister to the faithful, all without Father Dominic's guidance...

"We just don't know enough for such a work," declared Brother Matthew.

"We're only novices," Brother Oderic added. "How can we possibly teach others?"

Dominic smiled at the anxious faces before him. "In the next three months, through prayer and study, you'll learn all that is necessary," he said. "Wait and see."

But as summer came to Toulouse, the doubts at Saint Romanus became more pronounced than ever. By now Father Dominic had announced detailed plans for the future. On August 15, after making their vows as religious, seven of the brethren would go to Paris to establish a convent near the University. Four would go to Madrid, two would go to Prouille to care for the needs of the Sisters, and two would stay in Toulouse. As for the one member of the community remaining—Brother Stephen from Belgium—he would accompany Dominic on another trip to Rome.

When news of these plans spread, it caused as great consternation among friends and benefactors as it had done among members of the community. What could Father Dominic be thinking of, to disperse his little group so soon?

"My son, some of these followers of yours are a long way from finishing their studies for the priesthood," objected Bishop Foulques. "How can you possibly allow them to go out to preach and teach others—even to found monasteries?"

"Because there's no time to be lost, Your Lordship," replied Dominic.

"No time to be lost?"

"No. Heresy is everywhere. Europe needs preachers at once."

"But how can mere boys, eighteen and twenty years old. . ."

Dominic smiled. "These boys, as you call them, love God and the Blessed Mother, Your Lordship. I have every confidence in their abilities. Besides, they'll be living in Paris and Madrid, near the Universities. There'll be every chance there for them to go to school and complete their educations."

"While they lead the religious life?"

"Yes, Your Lordship."

The Bishop shook his head. "It's all very unusual," he said. "Personally, I think you're making a mistake—a fatal mistake."

Many others, including Count Simon de Montfort, shared the Bishop's sentiments. In fact, there was no one at all who sided with Dominic in the matter of dispersing his brethren so soon. Yet he was undismayed. Well he knew that book learning, important as it is, holds a far lower place in the salvation of souls than a knowledge and a love of God.

And a knowledge and a love of God can be acquired
by young people, even the very young, in an exceed-
ingly simple way.

"A little good reading, much prayer and medita-
tion," Dominic told his followers. "God will do the
rest."

Accordingly, the sixteen brethren set themselves
to follow Dominic's instructions. Each day they
read brief passages from the Gospels. Then they
went to the chapel to think of what they had read.
At first they had some trouble keeping their minds
fixed upon the matter at hand, but after a little
while the practice began to be easier. And strangely
enough, soon they found themselves becoming anxious for the brief period of holy reading and the
far longer period of thinking which had been made
part of their daily schedule. They began to ask
questions about this and that incident in the
Gospels, questions which had never occurred to
them before and which Father Dominic answered
simply and clearly.

"We *are* learning a great deal," declared Brother
Lawrence one day in a surprised tone of voice.
"Why, lately I find myself wondering about all sorts
of things. And I can't be satisfied until I find out
the answers."

"It's the same with me," put in Brother Michael.
"Why is it, Father Dominic?"

Dominic smiled at the expressions on the two
young faces before him. "It's because the Holy
Ghost is working in you," he said. "Since you began
to read and think upon the Gospels, He is working

in your souls in a new and wonderful way."

For a moment there was silence. Then Brother Lawrence looked up. "The Holy Ghost—He's the Spirit of Wisdom, isn't He, Father?"

Dominic nodded. "Yes, my son."

"And He's present in every soul in the state of grace?"

"That's right."

"But He's more active in our souls when we . . . well, when we think about the Word of God?"

Once again Dominic smiled. "Yes. That's why everyone, even children, can become really holy. All that is necessary is to remember the Divine Presence within yourself, to read good books, then call frequently upon the Holy Spirit for help in understanding and putting into practice what they contain."

"And the best book of all is the Bible?"

"Yes. But for your own needs just now, the Gospels in particular."

Nevertheless, when August arrived, the month appointed for the departure of Dominic's followers from Toulouse, they were ill at ease at the thought of going out upon their own. As for Bishop Foulques . . .

"The majority of your helpers are still unlettered men and boys," he declared soberly, as Dominic and he set out for Prouille, where the departure ceremony was to take place on the Feast of the Assumption. "Are you sure—*very sure*—that you're doing the wise thing in letting them go alone to Paris and Madrid?"

There was the usual peace in Dominic's eyes as he looked upon his good friend. "Your Lordship, please don't worry," he said. "Everything's going to be all right. I'm sure of it."

CHAPTER 8

THE FAMILY GROWS

AT PROUILLE, on August 15, Dominic received the religious vows of his little community. Then he once more announced his plans for the future. The Sisters were to remain cloistered, but the Brothers would go forth into the world. They would establish convents in the larger cities, particularly in the neighborhood of the great Universities. Here they would go to school themselves and mix with students and teachers in the effort to raise the standard of Christian living among them.

As they listened to their leader's ardent words, the sixteen found themselves filled with a courage which they had not known in several weeks. Indeed, it was a privilege to work for God in the new way described by Father Dominic. Why, if each of them made but one convert at the University of Paris...in the schools of Madrid and Toulouse...and then the converts in turn each won a soul for Christ...

"There's just one thing that bothers me,"

declared Brother John. "I've tried to put the thought away, but it keeps coming back."

Dominic looked up, smiling. "And what's that, my son?"

"How can we set out for Paris and Madrid without a cent to our names? Why, if one of us should get sick along the way, or if people should fail to give us alms. . ."

"I've told you many times that God will provide for you, just as He did for the Apostles."

"But it's a dreadful risky business, Father, depending on charity! I, for one, don't have enough faith."

A look of compassion crossed Dominic's face. Brother John was a good young man and a conscientious student, but he was of a highly practical turn of mind. From time to time he had even expressed the opinion that Brother Francis of Assisi must be a simpleton, to be so attached to Holy Poverty as to make no provisions for the future of himself and of his brethren.

"I'm afraid there's not much that I can say to help you," Dominic declared. "We've been over this matter so many times before."

"I know, Father."

"And just a short while ago you made a solemn promise, before God's altar, to obey me as superior of our family."

"I know that, too."

"Well, why not keep your promise? Go now and join your companions. You'll have a good trip to Paris, despite the lacks of funds."

After a moment's silence Brother John shook his head stubbornly. "I can't do it, Father! I just can't be a beggar!"

Suddenly Dominic realized what was happening. The devil was taking away a valuable helper by provoking him, Dominic, to anger! Brother John's lack of obedience merited a stern rebuke, and in a minute Dominic would probably punish him so severely that he would renounce his vow, leave the Order and thus fall into serious sin.

"But it mustn't be like this," he thought quickly. Then aloud: "You want money, my son? All right. I'll see that you have some for the trip to Paris."

Brother John was so taken aback by these words that for a moment he could not speak. Then tears filled his eyes, and he fell to his knees.

"You mean it, Father?"

"Of course I mean it."

"But. . .but I never expected. . ."

"Come, we'll see how much money there is in the treasury."

Within a few minutes all was settled. Brother John had a bag of coins to take with him to Paris. The total sum was not large, but at least it was something. However, when he and his companions had set out on their three-hundred-and-sixty-mile trip northwards, Dominic hurried to Our Lady's shrine. Humanly speaking, he was sad. He loved his young followers, and now they had gone from him. But there was another worry, too. He had saved Brother John's vocation, yet had he acted wisely in his method of doing so?

"Dearest Mother, please give all of us your blessing!" he begged. "As for Brother John—the poor boy's faith is so weak! Increase it, and make it really strong, so that never again will he doubt the Heavenly Father's love and protection!"

After the departure of his brethren, Dominic had hoped to leave at once for Rome with Brother Stephen. God willing, he would start a convent of the Order there, too. However, the arrival at Prouille of four new candidates—Brothers Arnold, Romeo, Poncio and Raymond—made it necessary to postpone the trip. The four were zealous young men, but quite ignorant of the religious life and in need of much training. Thus, it was not until late October of the year 1217 that the opportunity arose to journey to the Eternal City.

"How are we going to go to Rome?" asked Brother Stephen. "By south or north?"

Dominic hesitated. It would be quicker to follow the southern route—through Marseilles and other Mediterranean cities. But if he went the northern way, he could make a stop in Paris and see how his newly departed sons were faring.

"I think we'll take the longer route," he said finally. "Northern France has need of preachers, too."

In Paris, Dominic found that all was well with his friars. They had acquired a small house near the University, which they had placed under the patronage of Saint James, and here they were happily installed. According to instructions, each religious was also enrolled in the courses of theology and Scriptures at the University.

However, the decision to visit Paris eventually cost Dominic the companionship of his devoted follower, Brother Stephen. For upon pursuing his travels and arriving in the Belgian city of Metz, Stephen's birthplace, he found the people desperately eager for their fellow-citizen to remain with them. After all, Metz was in great need of preachers, too. And who was better suited to organize a group than Brother Stephen—himself a splendid speaker and an experienced missionary? Surely within a year or two he could even open a house of preaching friars...

"I agree with you," said Dominic. "Brother Stephen can do much good if he stays here in Metz."

Stephen had little confidence in his abilities, but he did not try to escape the task suddenly placed before him. A command from Dominic was as a command from God Himself. What matter that now he would never have the great joy of going to Rome with Dominic? Of spending long and happy hours in listening to his talks on Heaven, God, the Saints? There was work to be done in Metz— important work. And he was the one to whom it had been entrusted.

"I'll do my best to help people here, Father," he said. "But you—you will remember me in your prayers?"

Dominic nodded. "I'll remember you every day at God's altar," he assured him.

Within a short time Dominic was on his way

NEVER HAD ANYONE SEEN OR HEARD THE LIKE.

alone—taking advantage of his passing through the villages and towns of southern Germany to preach to the people. Naturally his garb of black and white wool attracted considerable attention, not to mention the wonderful eloquence with which he spoke. Never had anyone seen or heard the like. Who was he, anyway? Where had he come from? What were his plans?

Cheerfully Dominic answered the many questions put to him, blessed the sick and the children, heard Confessions and settled disputes when the occasion arose. Then one day he found himself confronted by four young men—Gregory, Henry, Albert and Otho. They had been so moved by a sermon which he had given in their village on the Blessed Mother that they had set aside their natural shyness and had come to ask questions.

"We never heard anyone speak so. . .so *convincingly* of Our Lady before," they declared. "Father, is everything that you said about her true?"

Dominic smiled at the serious young faces before him. "I do my best always to speak the truth, my sons."

"But you said that the Blessed Mother never fails to hear our prayers!"

"Yes, that's what I said."

"Well, I've often prayed to her for favors, Father, and she never gave them to me," observed Gregory.

Otho nodded. "And so have I—many times."

For a few moments Dominic seemed lost in thought. Then he turned to the young men. "Tell me what is the most valuable gift that anyone ever made you," he said quietly.

The four looked at one another in astonishment. Was Father Dominic joking? But no—his face was quite serious. And obviously he was waiting for a reply.

"I. . .well, my father is a rich man," volunteered Gregory. "On my eighteenth birthday he gave me a sword studded with rubies and emeralds. It cost a great deal of money."

Otho looked about thoughtfully. "My father isn't so rich," he admitted, "but last year he let me have his own horse—a splendid animal that can run like the wind. Believe me, I couldn't thank him enough for that."

Dominic smiled as he turned to Albert and Henry. "And you, my sons? What about your best gifts?"

The two hesitated, for they came from poor families, and had never received any presents to equal those described by Gregory and Otho. Nevertheless, with a little encouragement from Dominic, they set aside their shyness. Henry believed that his best gift was one which he had had since childhood—a good memory. It had served him so well at school that he was always first in his classes. As for Albert—well, he had never been sick a day in his life. And no one could surpass him in sports.

"I guess health is my best possession," he said.

Once again Dominic smiled. Then a serious expression crossed his face. "A fine sword, a swift horse, a keen memory, good health—all these *are* desirable things," he admitted. "And yet, my sons, do you know that they're really not your most precious possessions? Moreover, do you know that the best gift which any one of you has ever received is possessed by each of you? And by all other Christians as well?"

Puzzled, the four looked at one another. Then, before they could ask any questions, Dominic explained what he meant. The choicest gift in the world is the gift of salvation—the chance to go to Heaven when one dies! And through God's all-wise plan, this wonderful gift has come to us through His Mother!

"For our sakes, the Blessed Virgin said 'yes' at the Annunciation, my sons. Oh, how can we ever doubt her love for us when she made possible our Redemption? Or think that she fails to hear us when we pray to her for far lesser favors?"

In a little while the four were being carried out of themselves. Never had they heard such holy eloquence. This was the kind of talk by which Dominic had converted scores of French heretics and had given young men like themselves—average young men, who had never shown much interest in religious matters—a burning desire to consecrate themselves to Our Lady and then to do their part in bringing others to her and her Divine Son.

When Dominic had finished, Gregory looked up eagerly. His eyes were shining.

"Father, would it be possible. . .that is, do you think. . ."

Dominic smiled encouragingly. "Yes, my boy? What is it?"

"Could I come with you to Rome? I mean, could I be one of your friars?"

There was an awkward pause. Then one by one Gregory's companions hastened to ask the same questions. Would Father Dominic take them, too? Would he show them how to bring many souls to Heaven? Especially, would he teach them more about Our Lady?

For a long moment Dominic gazed upon their earnest faces. Then he stretched out both arms. "My sons," he murmured. *"My sons!"*

CHAPTER 9

THE YOUNG PROFESSOR

IN A FEW DAYS Dominic and his new companions were on their way, pushing steadily southwards through Germany and Switzerland and finally reaching Italy late in December. Stops were made at Milan, Venice and Bologna. Then early in January, 1218, the group arrived in Rome. Pope Honorius welcomed them warmly and lost no time in bestowing upon Dominic a most valuable gift— the Church of Saint Sixtus.

"It is a bit distant from the city, but it should make an ideal site for a monastery," he declared. Then, hesitating: "You do plan to have a house of your Order here?"

"Oh, yes, Your Holiness," Dominic replied. "That is why I have come. But of course I never dreamed..."

The Pope smiled. "If I have done you a favor, I expect one in return. Can you guess what it is?"

Dominic was at a loss to know what favor he, a poor traveling preacher, could do for Christ's vicar on earth. But presently everything was made clear.

Pope Honorius wanted the various communities of nuns living in Rome to be organized into one compact body—under a Rule such as that which was observed by the Sisters at Prouille.

"It won't be an easy task to unite the various convents," he warned. "Many of the Sisters will be against it, and their friends and families, too. But— well, will you try?"

Dominic did not hesitate. "Of course I'll try, Your Holiness. When do you wish me to start the work?"

Pope Honorius pondered. "You have plenty to do just now in setting your monastery of preachers in order," he said. "I think that it will be best to wait until the work at Saint Sixtus is well underway before doing anything about the Sisters."

"And I have your permission to preach in the city as I did before, Your Holiness?"

"Of course. And may God bless your labors in all ways."

Dominic lost no time in renewing old acquaintances in Rome. Each day found him preaching in one or another of the city's churches—urging his listeners to a more lively interest in their salvation. What mattered those things which until now had claimed their attention—money, health, friends, social position? In a few short years death would take all these away. It would bring them face to face with God Himself. Unless they had cultivated a sincere love for Him by using the graces given in this life, where would they be then? *What* would they be? Empty-handed fools, condemned to the most dreadful poverty possible—the eternal loss of Heaven!

"What a tragedy!" he cried. "Oh, while there's yet time, be wise! Ask the Heavenly Father for the grace to know Him, to love Him and to serve Him well upon this earth! Ask Our Lady to be with you at every moment! She has a mother's tender heart. She will give you the strength to triumph over sin—*if you ask her help every day!*"

So eagerly did Dominic urge a childlike confidence in the Blessed Virgin, especially in the devotion so close to her heart—her Psalter, or the Rosary, the one hundred and fifty Hail Marys said daily in her honor—that soon all Rome was feeling the effect. Lukewarm souls became aware of their spiritual laziness as never before and sought to make up for it. Hardened sinners came to kneel awkwardly at one or another of Our Lady's shrines—receiving there the grace to confess their faults and amend their lives. Devout men and women hastened to join the Confraternity which Dominic had established, thereby giving public notice that to the best of their abilities they would recite one hundred and fifty Hail Marys in honor of the Blessed Mother every day for the rest of their lives.

And at the new convent of Saint Sixtus near Rome even more marvels took place. Here, within a month of Dominic's arrival, no less than forty young men applied for admission as religious. Indeed, very soon it was being noised about the city that youths who even came within sight of Father Dominic were just about lost to friends and family. For a little while they might act as usual, pretending to be interested in this or that pleasure, but in the end

the strain would prove too great. They would be
off to Saint Sixtus, to beg the white woolen tunic,
linen surplice and black mantle of the Order of
Preachers.

"Father Dominic has some kind of holy magic,"
was the general opinion. "Young people—and
young men in particular—just can't keep away from
him."

But Dominic knew that he had no magic. The
secret of his success was that as a little child he
had offered himself to God to work for souls. Now
his prayer had been heard. He—a poor, human
creature—was being used as a tool by Divine Provi-
dence. For how long? Ah, there was no telling! He
was forty-eight years old. Possibly Heaven would
use him for many more years. Then again, perhaps
his period of usefulness would be a short one.
What did it matter, as long as God's Will was
accomplished?

"Heavenly Father, just let me be a good tool!"
he begged. "And let my helpers be good tools, too!"

Suddenly a specially gifted tool came Dominic's
way. This was Master Reginald of Orleans, a young
professor from the University of Paris, who was
stopping in Rome a few days on a pilgrimage to the
Holy Land. He was rich, learned, charming, with
a host of friends in Paris. Nevertheless, and despite
the promise of a brilliant career at the University,
he had never known real happiness.

"I certainly admire your life here," he admitted,
when Dominic had invited him to Saint Sixtus and
had shown him about the new monastery. "To

study, to preach, to go about among the people as your young followers are doing—it must be wonderful, Father!"

"Perhaps you'd like to join us?"

Reginald laughed lightly. "*I?* But I couldn't do that!"

"Why not?"

"I'm not one to give up all the good things of life!"

Dominic looked closely at his visitor. Master Reginald was about thirty years old—handsome, well-dressed, and with a ready wit and a carefree smile that made him appear exactly as he sounded —a man of the world. Yet behind the easy manners, the charm and brilliance that had made him the idol of all his students, Dominic sensed there was also a deeply serious mind. And just now, a troubled mind.

"My son, suppose you tell me your story," he suggested. "Perhaps I could help you."

Reginald flashed a brilliant smile and shook his head. "I haven't any story, Father. I'm merely a pilgrim on my way to the Holy Land. In a few months I'm due to return to my work in Paris. That's all."

"Ah, but why are you going to the Holy Land?"

The young professor's eyes clouded. "Well, I've a bit of a problem," he confessed. "I've been hoping that it will be solved when I kneel at the Holy Sepulcher."

"So I thought. And the problem deals with your future, doesn't it?"

"Y-yes."

"Shall I tell you what it is?"

"Oh, but you can't possibly know. . ."

"Briefly, it is this. The Lord has given you a good mind, health, money, friends, success. For several years you've been doing fine work among the students at the University. But it hasn't really brought you peace. You want something more. And your good mind tells you that the only way to find this 'something more' is to give yourself and your gifts to God's service. *And at once!*"

Dominic's words had an extraordinary effect upon the young professor. Suddenly he set aside all pretense, and with tears in his eyes admitted their truth. For years he had been struggling for courage to leave the world and give himself to God. But the very thought of entering a monastery, of being tied down to one place, of renouncing his own will in favor of that of a superior, had appalled him. Then, too, there were the responsibilities of the priesthood. How could he—who so loved the good things of life—ever hope to persevere in such a holy calling?

"But it's different now," he exclaimed. "Father, with God's help, I think I can do it! Will you let me come to Saint Sixtus? Will you show me how to give myself to Him as one of your preachers?"

Dominic's eyes glowed. "Of course, my son. God be praised for the grace that He's given you today!"

But Reginald's struggle with the powers of darkness was far from being over. Scarcely had he left Dominic's presence when all his former doubts returned. His work in Paris, his friends, his comfortable way of living—how could he even dream of renouncing them forever? Perhaps if he were younger, it might be different. But he was thirty years old, not a mere boy. His habits were set, and it would be very hard to form new ones. Besides, was it really necessary? He had been leading a good life in Paris—far more so than many of the others at the University. Surely he could save his soul without becoming a religious?

When Dominic saw how things were going, he redoubled his prayers and sacrifices in Reginald's behalf, and urged his community to do the same. What wonderful things grace could accomplish in souls through the young Frenchman, once he was one of them! With such learning and brilliance, such power for good over the young . . .

"We mustn't let this soul escape us," he insisted. "No matter what it costs!"

Then one day there was great consternation at Saint Sixtus. Master Reginald had fallen victim to the fever and was very ill!

"The young man is worried about something," the doctor told Dominic. "At times his mind is clear, then it wanders. He keeps talking about not being worthy of some grace, of falling into sin and losing his soul."

"But surely he's going to recover?"

The doctor hesitated. "I don't know. Whatever is worrying him is using up all his strength. And that's not good. Not good at all."

Reginald's condition grew steadily worse, and the spirits of all at Saint Sixtus were low. How dreadful to lose this valuable brother—*and especially before he had made his vows as a religious!*

Dominic's own feelings were kept well hidden on his visits to Reginald's bedside. "You mustn't worry," he urged over and over again. "Our Lady will see that everything turns out all right. If you wish, you can become one of us right now. Just repeat these words after me. . ."

But Reginald shook his head. "I'm not worthy," he murmured. "I can't accept the honor of dying as a religious. . .when I've never done anything to earn it. . ."

Dominic did not lose heart. Well he knew that prayer and suffering have an extraordinary power to win graces for others, and so he continued his pleading that the son so dear to him should be spared—even if only for a little while. His faith was rewarded, for one morning when he came to visit Reginald he found him sitting up in bed with a tinge of fresh color in his cheeks.

"Father, I'm cured!" the young professor announced. "Our Lady's been here and made me well!"

Dominic looked closely at this young man for whom so many prayers and sacrifices had been offered, then clasped his hands. "Tell me everything!" he cried. "When did it happen? *How* did it happen?"

"It was about an hour ago, Father. I was burning up with such a dreadful fever that I felt all would be over very soon. I couldn't possibly suffer any more and still live."

"Yes, yes! Go on!"

"Suddenly I saw the Blessed Mother. She was young and beautiful, and with such a gracious smile—oh, I can't describe it!"

"She spoke to you?"

"Yes. She asked me to tell her what I wanted most in the whole world, and she would give it to me."

"You asked to be cured!"

"No, Father. I couldn't make up my mind what to ask. But there were two beautiful maidens with Our Lady, and one of them suggested that I place myself in the hands of the Queen of Heaven. She would do for me what was best."

"You agreed?"

"Yes. And Our Lady seemed pleased at this. She came over to me, anointed me with some kind of oil, prayed over me for a little while, then told me to be of good heart. It was God's Will that I become a preaching friar at Saint Sixtus. With her help I would be able to persevere."

"And after that?"

"Oh, something very strange, Father!"

"Strange?"

"Yes. Our Lady showed me a scapular of white wool. 'Behold the habit of your Order,' she said. Then, as I looked at the scapular, she and her two companions departed. When I finally came to my senses, the fever was gone and I knew myself to be cured."

Dominic gazed joyfully upon his young companion. There was no doubt about it. Reginald *was*

cured. In a miraculous fashion Our Lady had
restored his health. But the other wonder which
she had performed—the vision of the scapular of
white wool—what could it possibly mean? And the
words which she had spoken: "Behold the habit of
your Order..."

He leaned forward impulsively. "Shall we thank
the Blessed Mother for what she has done today?
And shall we ask her to tell us the meaning of that
scapular of white wool?"

Reginald's eyes shone. "Oh, yes, Father!"

So the two began the beautiful prayer which of
late everyone in Rome had come to love: *"Hail
Mary, full of grace, the Lord is with thee, blessed
art thou among women..."*

"BEHOLD THE HABIT OF YOUR ORDER."

CHAPTER 10

LIFE AT SAINT SIXTUS

THREE DAYS LATER, when Dominic was once more visiting with Reginald, all was made plain. The vision described by the young professor occurred again. And this time, since Dominic witnessed Our Lady bestowing the white woolen scapular upon his companion, he understood what must be done. Henceforth the Brothers and Sisters of the Order of Preachers should wear a similar scapular, and regard it as the holiest part of their habit. For it was truly a gift from Heaven, a sign of Our Lady's interest in their welfare.

"You will be the first to receive this holy emblem," Dominic told Reginald joyfully. "May God keep you ever worthy to wear it!"

Of course there was great rejoicing at Saint Sixtus over the young professor's cure, not to mention the fact that Our Lady had given her personal approval of the Order of Preachers. On the day chosen by Dominic, the friars doffed the linen surplices which they had been wearing over their woolen tunics and reverently replaced them with the new scapular. From now on they would merit in a special way the title which so many gave them—"The Brothers of Mary."

As for Reginald? After receiving him into the Order, Dominic permitted him to continue his pilgrimage to the Holy Land—for the young professor had bound himself by vow to make the trip. Later in the year he would return to Saint Sixtus for his religious training. Then, God willing, he would go to Bologna to help found still another community of preaching friars.

"That city has the most famous law school in Europe," Dominic told himself eagerly. "What great good Brother Reginald will be able to do among the teachers and students there!"

But while his heart rejoiced at the thought that many keen minds might be touched by grace to seek entrance into the Order, Dominic did not lose sight of present problems. There were now more than forty young men at Saint Sixtus, each eager to become a preaching friar. What an enormous task to train them as religious, then send them forth well equipped for their life's work!

But presently a problem of quite another nature occurred. The young friar in charge of the kitchen at Saint Sixtus came to Dominic one day and announced that the larder was bare—save for a few hard crusts.

"It's never happened before, Father!" he cried. "Always those Brothers who go out begging have brought home a little something...bread, or cheese, or a few vegetables at least. But this time. . ."

Dominic put his hand upon the young man's shoulder. "This time the Brothers didn't bring home anything?"

"No, Father. What are we going to do?"

"Well, it's almost noon. I think that what we'll do is to ring the bell for dinner."

In a few minutes the community had assembled in the refectory. But just as they were seated before their empty plates, two strange young men entered the room, carrying a quantity of freshly baked loaves, which they began to distribute to all present.

Believing the newcomers to be the servants of some wealthy family, the community received the loaves gratefully, but without too much surprise. However, when the young men had finished serving, they vanished from where they stood. Then there was awed astonishment in every heart. *Could it be that the young men were angels?*

"Yes," Dominic said. "Oh, how good God is to those who trust in Him!"

Word of the miracle soon spread far and wide. Now people of every age and station flocked to hear Dominic's sermons in the Church of Saint Mark and elsewhere in Rome.

"Father Dominic is a saint!" they declared. "Why, at his prayers the very angels in Heaven come to help his community!"

"That's right. Even his shadow can cure the sick."

Everyone wanted a relic of the wonderworker, and whenever he appeared in the streets there was a mad rush to obtain some kind of souvenir. Over-zealous fingers even cut pieces from his habit, much to the distress of the brethren at Saint Sixtus.

"Father, people have no right to touch you, much less to push and shove and all but cut your habit into shreds," they complained. "Won't you let us give them a good lesson—one that they won't forget for a long time?"

Dominic smiled at his young followers, many of them well equipped to give a good account of themselves in a crowd. "No," he said. "People don't mean any harm. And if a little piece of woolen cloth will help to turn their thoughts to God and give them love and confidence in Him—well, let them have it."

So men, women and children continued to follow Dominic wherever he went, begging for his bless-ing and pressing as close as possible when he preached from the pulpit or in the open air. Later, they joined in the hymns and prayers which he offered, their hearts filled with a zeal and fervor which they never knew when they prayed alone.

Then one day excitement spread like wildfire through the streets of the city. _Father Dominic had raised the dead to life!_ One of his most faith-ful followers—a woman named Gutadona—had returned home from hearing his sermon at the Church of Saint Mark to find her only son dead. When the first shock of her grief was over, she had ordered the lifeless body carried to the Monastery

FATHER DOMINIC HAD RAISED THE DEAD TO LIFE!

of Saint Sixtus. She had pleaded with Father Dominic and. . .

"He just made the Sign of the Cross, took the boy's hand in his, and raised him to his feet," Brother Tancred explained to those who had not witnessed the miracle. "Oh, how good it was to see the boy speak to his mother!"

"But surely there was more to it than that!" cried Brother Philip, a newcomer to Saint Sixtus, unbelievingly. "Didn't Father Dominic say some long prayers? Or at least some special ones?"

Brother Tancred shook his head. "No, it was all quite simple. He just recollected himself a moment, then made the Sign of the Cross."

"Slowly and fervently, and with a little smile?"

"Yes, that's the way it was!" burst out Brother Gregory. "As though he expected something nice to happen!"

Brother Philip hesitated. "I. . . I've often noticed how Father Dominic makes the Sign of the Cross," he said shyly. "In fact, it's that which first attracted me to him."

At the young novice's words, the members of the little group looked at one another. How true! Father Dominic did make the Sign of the Cross in a manner not usual to other people. . .

"He seems to be. . .well, *seeing* something as he makes it," observed Brother Sixtus after a moment. "And *thinking*, too."

"Yes. And have you noticed how many times a day he makes it?"

"Oh, it must be dozens of times!"

"Yes, and as carefully and lovingly each time."

For a moment no one spoke. Then Brother Tancred turned thoughtfully to his companions. "Suppose that in the future we try to make the Sign of the Cross with real devotion," he suggested. "You know, it could mean the meriting of many new graces which the Lord has been wanting to give us for a long time."

"Yes!" cried Brother Philip. "Let's try!"

So it was agreed. And as the days passed, the wonder caused by Dominic's miracle of raising the dead boy to life was no greater than that aroused by the fresh insight which his followers were receiving into the extraordinary power for good in a simple prayer which they had known since childhood but had never really appreciated until now—the Sign of the Cross.

"When we go out to preach, we must tell everyone about it," they decided. "So few people ever take the trouble to offer it properly."

"Yes, and what a pity! For the Sign of the Cross is very easy to make and to say—even for the sick and old people."

"That's right. And it's not too hard for children, either—even very small children."

To Dominic, his disciples' devotion to the Sign of the Cross was a companion-grace to the wonder God had permitted him to perform for Gutadona's son, and he was greatly encouraged. But as the weeks of 1218 slipped by, he realized with some anxiety that very soon he must leave Saint Sixtus. It was going to take much time and labor to estab-

lish his friars in Bologna. Also, he ought to return
to France to see what progress was being made in
the houses of the Order there. Then, too, what
about Spain? From all accounts, things were not
going so well for the brethren...

"I shall leave for Bologna in October," he told
the community one day, "and from there for Paris
and Madrid."

Hearts were heavy at this announcement,
although everyone understood that Father Dominic
really had to go. He had been in Rome for several
months now, and of course he was needed elsewhere. Then one morning, shortly before the date
set for his departure, Dominic found himself face
to face with worried novices—Brothers John and
Albert. It seemed that they had been sent out some
hours earlier to beg for the community. But what
poor luck they had had! In all their travels they had
come across only one person to give them an alms.
This had been a poor widow with a small loaf of
bread.

"Then we met a beggar, Father," said Brother
Albert forlornly. "He was dressed in rags, and was
in a terrible state."

"That's right," put in Brother John, shuddering.
"It was near the Church of Saint Anastasia. And
the beggar looked at our one small loaf so
longingly..."

"Of course we explained that it was all we
had..."

"But he kept looking at it, and his life story was
so pitiful..."

"Finally we said to ourselves: 'What can we do with just one little loaf? Let us give it to him for the love of God.'"

"And you did?"

"Yes, Father."

"And now you have nothing?"

"Nothing, Father."

For a moment there was silence. Then Dominic bade the two young men to be of good heart. The Lord had looked after them in the past. He would not fail to do so again.

"Come into the church for a moment," he said. "After that, go and ring the bell for dinner."

The novices looked at each other in astonishment. *Dinner?* How could there be any dinner? And yet, Father Dominic did not seem troubled. In fact, he seemed quite pleased at the way in which things had turned out...

CHAPTER 11

IN BOLOGNA

IN A SHORT WHILE Dominic's confidence in assembling the community was justified. As they took their places at the bare wooden tables in the refectory, there was a sudden stir, and two young men in white garments entered the room. Each carried a supply of freshly baked loaves in a linen cloth which hung from his shoulders before and behind. And in silence, with many gracious smiles and nods, they began to distribute the loaves.

"Angels!" everyone thought. "The angels have come again!"

But no one spoke, only sat open-mouthed as the visitors went about the task of distributing the warm, fragrant loaves. For they did not, as before, serve Dominic first, then the younger members of the community. This time they began with the lay Brothers and the novices (who were seated at the lower ends of the tables, which were arranged in horseshoe fashion). Then they progressed to the older friars; and, having reached Dominic's place,

THEY SET THE LAST LOAF BEFORE HIM.

they set the last loaf before him and vanished.
For a long moment the awed silence in the refectory remained unbroken. Then Dominic spoke.
"Let us eat the bread which the Lord has sent."
Of course for the rest of the day no one could
talk of anything but this second visit of the angels.
How wonderful it all was! How...how *unbelievable!* For although everyone had eaten his fill of the
heavenly bread, at the end of the meal there had
been just as much left on the table as at the beginning. And the same with the wine. No matter how
much was drawn from the wine casks, an ample
supply remained.

"It's wine of the best quality, too," observed
Brother Roger. (He was frequently in charge of food
supplies at Saint Sixtus, and knew good wine when
he tasted it.) "God be praised!"

But this was only the beginning. On the second
day, and again on the third, the miraculous bread
and wine were still renewing themselves at Saint
Sixtus, so that the friars did not have to go out on
their usual begging trips. However, fearful lest he
and his brethren should forget the meaning of holy
poverty, Dominic finally announced that the
heavenly food must be removed from the house and
distributed to the poor.

"I think we have all learned our lesson," he said.
"The Lord provided for us so wonderfully because
we trusted in Him—*and because two of our brethren did not turn away from a beggar when they
might easily have done so!*"

Then, to prevent future generations of preaching

friars from forgetting the great beauty of charity to the poor, a new custom was decided upon. Henceforth the lay Brothers and the novices would be served first at mealtime—in direct contradiction to the tradition prevailing in other monastic houses. In this way the remembrance of the angels' visit to Saint Sixtus would be forever celebrated in all convents of the Order.

Not long after this, Dominic left Rome for Bologna. He had been there earlier in the year, around Pentecost Sunday, when he had visited with Brother Francis of Assisi and attended a General Chapter of the Order of Friars Minor. But now his thoughts were far from those happy days. Indeed, he found himself somewhat discouraged. For though a few of his disciples had been living in Bologna for some months, they had made almost no headway in establishing a convent of the Order. True, they did have a headquarters—the Church of Saint Mary of Mascarella—but the place was small and inconveniently situated, and not many people attended the services.

"We need a much larger church," Dominic decided. "And above all, because of the University, we need a man in charge who can really preach . . . and who knows and loves young people."

There were several friars at Saint Sixtus who possessed these qualities, but deep in his heart Dominic knew that only one would make a real success of the work at Bologna. This was Brother Reginald of Orleans, who had taught so successfully at Paris and whom the Blessed Mother had cured of the fever not so many months ago, giving him the scapular of the Order. Thank God that he was now on his way back from Jerusalem, having fulfilled his vow to visit the Holy Land.

"Hasten his steps, O Lord!" Dominic prayed fervently. "Only when he comes will I feel safe in leaving for France and Spain."

Reginald arrived in Bologna in November, 1218, scarcely a month after Dominic. And although he felt a great reluctance to accept complete charge of the preaching at Saint Mary of Mascarella (well he knew that he belonged with the other novices at Saint Sixtus, rather than in a position of authority), he accepted the responsibilities laid upon him.

"You can do wonderful work here," Dominic told him confidently, explaining how the University in Bologna had the most famous law school in all Europe, and that undoubtedly there were scores of students there who would make fine recruits for the Order. "Oh, my son! Pray, then preach to these young people as you've never preached before!"

"Yes, Father," said Reginald.

But when Dominic had taken his departure (he was scheduled to visit the brethren in Toulouse and Prouille, then journey down to Segovia, in Spain, where efforts to establish a house of the Order had met with no success), Reginald's heart grew heavy. What an impossible situation! He, who should be learning about the religious life, was himself expected to tell others about it! Even more. He was expected to found a monastery of preachers at Bologna—and this when other friars, far more experienced than he, had failed!

"Dear Blessed Mother, how can I do these things?" he asked desperately. "How can I bring young men to give themselves to your Son? How can I even get them to this little church to listen to me?"

At first there seemed to be no answer to these questions. But remembering that he was now a friar, and bound by vow to holy obedience, Reginald refused to be discouraged for long. What matter if only a few people troubled to visit Saint Mary of Mascarella? Surely if just one of these could be brought to greater holiness by his words, his efforts would be well worthwhile?

"Dearest Mother, I shall tell about you," he declared, "and that prayer which is so often on the lips of our Father Dominic—the Hail Mary."

The decision was a wise one. Reginald's sermons on Our Lady, short and simple though they were, had a powerful influence on the little groups who heard them, and in just a short time men and women were flocking to Saint Mary's in unbelievable numbers.

"Brother Reginald is the best preacher we've had in Bologna in a long time," was the general opinion.

"That's right. And to think that he's actually seen the Blessed Mother!"

"And talked with her, too!"

"The Blessed Mother?"

"Yes. Didn't you know? She appeared to him a few months ago and cured him of a grievous illness."

"It was down in Rome, and he was at death's door."

"But...but that's a miracle!"

"Of course it's a miracle. Brother Reginald almost weeps when he tells about it."

As the details of Reginald's cure became more widely known, including the story of how the Queen of Heaven had given him the white woolen scapular, interest in the Order of Preachers reached new heights. What a wonderful man was Brother Reginald! One could listen to his preaching for hours!

"It's as though Saint Paul himself had returned to earth," said one man.

"Or the prophet Elias," put in another.

Then, as Dominic had hoped and prayed, a few University students drifted to Saint Mary's out of sheer curiosity. In their classrooms they had heard of Master Reginald of Orleans, the celebrated scholar from the University of Paris. But how was it possible, they asked themselves, that he and the black-and-white-clad friar now preaching in their city were one and the same person? Rumor had it that Master Reginald had never been averse to the good things of life. For years his well-furnished house in Paris had been the meeting place for people who were far from being saints—poets, musicians, artists, scholars of every description. It had been the aim of most young intellectuals to be admitted to this group for the valuable connections which later would lead, not to the cloister, but to an interesting and prosperous career in the world.

Now how did all this fit in with Reginald's present labors? How was it that he had left a promising future at the most famous University in Europe for a life of prayer and penance in a religious Order? An Order, moreover, where even the most intellectual or highly born member was required to beg for his daily food?

Reginald's heart beat fast at the sight of the students in the congregation, and he lost no time in answering the unspoken questions in their eyes. Standing in the pulpit, an imposing figure in his black and white habit, he threw wide his arms as though to embrace the whole world.

"I am here because I am learning to love!" he cried.

CHAPTER 12

A DAUGHTER FOR DOMINIC

BY JANUARY OF the year 1219—only two months after Reginald's arrival in Bologna— it was evident that he and his preaching friars must do something, and very quickly, about acquiring larger quarters. The Church of Saint Mary of Mascarella was far too small, not to mention the convent attached to it. Yet despite all this, scarcely a day passed when some University student did not come to beg for admission into the community. As for the crowds at the daily sermons...

"There's never been anything like it before," observed the people of Bologna. "Even Father Dominic didn't attract the young folks as does Master Reginald of Orleans!"

It was true. Master Reginald (now simply Brother Reginald of the Order of Preachers) was working wonders. Lukewarm souls had only to hear him speak once about heavenly things when such a love for God would fill their hearts that they could not be satisfied with their way of life. They must do something for the Lord, by a gift of their services, their possessions, or themselves. *And at once!* In fact, shortly after Reginald's arrival in Bologna some of the most learned professors at the University admitted that they would end their days wearing the black and white habit of a preaching friar. It was as though Reginald were a magnet, and they themselves but fragments of steel.

There was one of Reginald's listeners, however, who dared to hope for nothing more than an occasional word with him. This was seventeen-year-old Diana d'Andalò, whose family owned considerable property in Bologna. At first she had attended the sermons at Saint Mary's out of curiosity. Then like everyone else she had fallen captive to Reginald's eloquence. Now with her whole heart she yearned to be a member of Dominic's family. But how could she? As yet only the preaching friars had come to her native city. And as for being one of the cloistered nuns in far-away Prouille...

"I'd never be holy enough for that," she said regretfully on the day of her first meeting with Reginald.

He looked closely at his unexpected visitor. Most of those who arranged to see him after his sermons were men and boys from the University. And usually their problems were quickly settled, either by acceptance or rejection for membership in the Order of Preachers. But this girl—young, beautiful, undoubtedly the heiress to considerable wealth—what about her? Plainly she had a soul capable of great things. And more than ordinary intelligence.

"Who is your spiritual director?" he asked.

Diana hesitated, her dark eyes aglow with eagerness. "No one, Brother Reginald."

"*No one?*"

"No. You see, I've never been interested in the spiritual life. But since listening to your sermons—"

"Things have started to change?"

"Y-yes."

"Now you find yourself thinking about death, and the emptiness of this life unless it is given over to God's service?"

"Oh, yes! I think about these things all the time. And...and I don't know what to do!"

Reginald smiled. "Suppose that you come to see me each week, and we'll have a talk," he said. "Who knows? Perhaps we can help each other to be better servants of the Lord."

Diana was overjoyed at Reginald's interest in her welfare, and before long had shown her appreciation in a most useful way. She prevailed upon her grandfather, Peter de Lovello, to grant the preaching friars the right to use a piece of poverty which had been in the family for generations—the Church of Saint Nicholas in the Vineyards, with all adjoining land. The place was at some distance from the city, but this was really an advantage, since it meant that the friars could enjoy the peace and quiet of the countryside while remaining in contact with life in Bologna. They could also plan on building a convent large enough to accommodate all the vocations which had developed since Reginald's arrival.

"Oh, Grandfather, how good you are!" cried

Diana when the necessary papers were completed. "Now the friars have a proper home at last!"

"Humph!" grunted Peter, shrugging his shoulders. "I hope I don't live to regret this day."

Diana's eyes widened. "But Grandfather! I thought. . ."

"My dear, I've let you influence me far more than you know. These preaching friars in black and white—well, I'm afraid that I haven't so very much use for them."

"*Grandfather!*"

"Why able-bodied men should go out begging for land and buildings, even for the very food they eat, when with proper planning they could have plenty of security. . ."

"But I explained all about that, Grandfather! The friars practice poverty for the love of God. They want to show their dependence on Him."

"Dependence! There are plenty of holy religious who would never think of roaming from door to door like common beggars. Or of stirring up the people with new-fangled sermons."

Diana sighed. Well she knew that her father and brothers shared these sentiments, and that it was little short of a miracle that her grandfather had allowed Reginald and his friars the use of the Church of Saint Nicholas. But then her heart lightened somewhat. Her spiritual guide had worked so many wonders with his words! Surely he could work another, and win the trust and affection of her family?

"Make it so, dear Lord!" she prayed. "And soon!"

But in August, 1219, only three months after the friars had taken over their new home, Dominic returned from his travels through France and Spain with word that Reginald was needed in Paris. He had done a splendid work in establishing the Order in Bologna, but now he must not be content with that. A gift for leadership such as he possessed should be put to the best possible use. And surely at the Monastery of Saint James, close to the most famous University in Europe. . .

"My son, you will be able to do great things in Paris," he said. "And how glad your friends will be to see you again!"

"Yes, Father," said Reginald.

But Diana did not receive the news so calmly. In fact, she wept bitter tears that the spiritual guide whom she had known but a few months was to be taken from her. What would she do without him? By now she was almost certain that God was calling her to the religious life—perhaps even to play some part in establishing a convent of Dominic's nuns in Bologna. But how to do these things alone and unaided, especially when her family was sternly set against the idea?

"Tell me all about it," said Dominic when Diana sought him out for advice. "Perhaps I could help."

So Diana poured out her story—how she was not yet eighteen years of age, how she had been led by Reginald's sermons to desire a more perfect Christian life, how he had helped her during the last few months to a better knowledge and love of God, until now—despite the objections and even

SHE SOLEMNLY GAVE HERSELF TO GOD.

the threats of her family—her great desire was to give herself to God in the religious life.

"But child, you can serve God, and in the special way which you desire, while still remaining in the world," said Dominic. Then, after a pause: "Of course you understand what I mean?"

Diana nodded. "You mean that I could make a solemn promise to give my heart to God alone, Father."

"Yes, that's right."

"But...but it's not enough! I want to give God everything! Not just my love, but everything that I own—or may own—some day! I want to serve Him as you do...as a real religious!"

Dominic smiled. How many times he had heard these generous words, especially from the lips of young men! And how many times he had welcomed the speakers into his little family—in Prouille, in Toulouse, in Paris, in Rome—and more recently in the Spanish cities of Segovia and Madrid!

But Diana was a girl, and as yet no provisions had been made for a convent of nuns in Bologna...

"Child, in spiritual matters it is usually best to make haste slowly," he said thoughtfully. "I think that for the time being the Lord will be satisfied with your promise to give your heart to Him alone. Later, perhaps, you will make Him the other gifts of a true religious."

So, on a day chosen by Dominic, Diana came to the Church of Saint Nicholas. Kneeling before the high altar, in the presence of Brothers Reginald, Guala and Rudolph, she solemnly gave herself to God:

> "I, Diana d'Andalò, a poor miserable sinner, out of
> pure love for Jesus Christ, in Whose mercy and pro-
> tection I place all my confidence and strength, of my
> full and entire free will, without any constraint
> whatever, choose this day this same Saviour for my
> spouse; and in pledge of this spiritual contract here
> consecrate myself to the Lord until death . . ."

Suddenly Dominic's heart gave a great leap. By
a miracle of grace he was looking into the future!
And what a terrifying, yet consoling, sight met his
eyes! Within a year's time the girl kneeling before
him would be called upon to endure the most terrible sufferings! While awaiting the establishment in
Bologna of a convent of Dominic's own daughters,
she would secretly enter the Augustinian convent
at Ronzano, on the outskirts of the city, only to be
dragged out some days later by her angry father and
brothers and permanently crippled in the struggle!

Yet she would not be unfaithful to her promise
never to give her heart to a mere creature. Indeed,
she would eventually win the understanding of her
family, and with their help play an important part
in establishing the Order's first house for women
in Bologna. Even more. Some day, with the joy and
confidence of little children, the entire Order of
Preachers would call upon her thus:

Pray for us, Blessed Diana!

That we may be made worthy of the promises of
Christ!

CHAPTER 13

A NEW WORK

DURING THE REMAINING weeks of his stay in Bologna, Dominic frequently impressed upon his young friend the great value of the grace which had been granted to her. Through no merit of her own she had been inspired to give her heart to God! From now on she would love all creatures *in Him,* and so escape the disappointment which so many must suffer on finding that the things of this world are not always what they seem.

Then one day, remembering the vision which he had been granted of Diana's future, Dominic began to speak about still another grace.

"Child, only a very few people ever think to ask the Lord for a love of suffering," he said thoughtfully. "And what a pity it is!"

Diana looked up questioningly. "A pity, Father?"

"Yes. For instance, haven't you ever wondered what it is that makes life so unbearable at times?"

"Well—"

"It's suffering, isn't it? Or even just the fear of it?"

"I . . . I suppose so, Father."

"Ah, you know that it is! So why not ask Our Lord to give you a love of suffering—yes, even a real thirst for it?"

Diana shuddered. "But I'd be too afraid, Father."

"*Afraid?*"

"Yes, Father."

"Listen. In this world suffering comes to everyone. So why not be ready for it? Even more. Why not pray to see it for the blessing that it is?"

In awed silence Diana stared at the black-and-white-clad figure before her. Of course she had always known, in a vague kind of way, that holiness depends in large measure upon the willingness to suffer. But in the past this very knowledge had been enough to make her hold back from even attempting to be a saint. After all, how hard to welcome suffering when all about are people, even very good people, who do their best to avoid it! Yet now. . .

"Don't worry," said Dominic, reading her thoughts. "Anyone, even a coward, can learn to love suffering—*if only he will ask God's help every day!*"

Then, to Diana's amazement, Dominic began to speak in such terms of the power of the cross—humbly accepted—to do good for others, that she was carried out of herself. Somehow she found herself setting aside her fears and asking the Lord for what she had never dreamed of asking in all her eighteen years: a love, and even a desire, for suffering!

Of course Dominic was overjoyed that his young friend had taken this all-important step on the road to holiness. Who knew? Perhaps in time she would be able to influence others to follow in her footsteps. Then countless souls would find themselves reaching out for God—*and finding Him*—as never before!

But although Dominic rejoiced at the new grace given to Diana, he was unable to stay longer in Bologna to watch its result. Having made the final arrangements for Reginald's departure for Paris immediately after Christmas, he himself set out to observe the feast in Rome.

"It's been more than eighteen months since I left Saint Sixtus," he thought. "I wonder what's been happening there all this time?"

Seasoned traveler that he was, Dominic had soon covered the two hundred miles from Bologna to Rome, discovering to his great joy that much good had been accomplished by the brethren during his absence. For instance, there had been several new vocations to the Order, so that now the community at Saint Sixtus numbered more than a hundred. Again, through the efforts of certain of the brethren, the people of Rome were acquiring a still greater love of the Blessed Mother, with scores pledged to the daily recitation of her Psalter.

All too soon, however, Dominic discovered that there was also some criticism of his friars and their work. In fact, in one quarter there was downright opposition.

"It comes from the nuns, Father," said Brother Tancred sadly. "They're. . .well, they're terribly suspicious of us."

"Suspicious?"

"Yes, Father," said Brother Albert. "Particularly those living in the Monastery of Saint Mary across the Tiber."

Some two years ago Pope Honorius had entrusted to Dominic the task of uniting all the convents of Rome under the Rule which had been written for the nuns at Prouille. In fact, it was really in recognition of the work involved that the Holy Father had given him the Monastery of Saint Sixtus. So far, of course, because of the press of other duties, he had not been able to attend to this. But now. . .

"I suppose that some of the Sisters are afraid our Rule is too hard," he ventured. "Especially the part about keeping a strict cloister."

Brother Tancred agreed. "That's right, Father. In fact, a few of the more outspoken ones—and particularly their friends and relations living here in Rome—say that they will make trouble for you if you attempt even the smallest change in the Sisters' way of life."

In a few days Dominic was experiencing the truth of these words. The various communities of nuns in Rome were not at all interested in adopting the Rule of an almost unheard-of convent in France —Our Lady of Prouille. How ridiculous, they declared, for noble-born Italian women to work at spinning and weaving like ordinary peasants! To sleep on beds which were little more than rough planks! To fast the greater part of the year! To wear coarse woolen habits! To possess nothing of their own! To come together for prayer at midnight and other unreasonable hours! Above all, never to go home for a visit with family and friends...

"I, for one, won't have anything to do with these new practices," said Mother Eugenia emphatically. (She was the superior of the Monastery of Saint Mary across the Tiber—one of the largest convents for women in Rome.) "They may be all very well for certain types of religious, but for us they're unnecessary. And impractical, too."

"Impractical?" echoed several of the older Sisters in relief. "Why, dearest Mother, they're downright imprudent!"

As the days passed, matters went from bad to worse, for Pope Honorius announced that he had given the preaching friars a new headquarters for their work. This was one-half of his family palace adjoining the ancient Church of Santa Sabina. When the friars had moved here, he said, it was his hope that the various Sisterhoods of the city— with the nuns of Saint Mary's leading the way— would band together peaceably and come to live at Saint Sixtus under the Rule which Dominic had written for his daughters at Prouille. Such an arrangement would surely make for better order, as well as for the spiritual good of all concerned.

"But why should we leave Saint Mary's?" objected Mother Eugenia. "It's always been our home!"

"And why should other nuns come to live with us?" demanded her followers. "They're probably not our sort at all."

DOMINIC PRAYED EARNESTLY
ABOUT THE PROBLEM.

"And the new Rule—oh, it's far too hard to keep!"

"That's right. Not even one little piece of meat a year!"

Dominic prayed long and earnestly about the problem at hand, then determined to visit the nuns of Saint Mary's. God willing, he might be able to settle at least some of the difficulties involved. And perhaps—oh, happy thought!—he could even reach a complete understanding with Mother Eugenia and her companions.

So it was (and with the utmost kindness) that presently he was pointing out to the community the great need for a reform in the convents of Rome if each Sister was to reach the degree of perfection which God required of her. Then he proceeded to describe the many abuses existing, and how all could be changed if only the nuns of Saint Mary's would set an example by coming to Saint Sixtus and promising to live under the Rule in force at Prouille. Then there would be but one type of religious life for women in all Rome—a holy life, stressing the beauty of prayer and penance.

Alas! Mother Eugenia was completely unmoved by Dominic's pleading, likewise her companions. "What you ask is impossible, Father, and for many reasons," she said firmly. "But especially because of the picture."

"*The picture?*"

"Yes, Father. The picture of Our Lady painted by Saint Luke. It's our greatest treasure. We just couldn't part with it."

Dominic's eyes widened. "But there's no question of your parting with a picture!" he exclaimed. "Why, you are more than welcome..."

Mother Eugenia shook her head. "You don't understand, Father. Our beautiful painting belongs here. And nowhere else."

Then, to Dominic's amazement, Mother Eugenia began to unfold the startling tale of how, more than three centuries ago, Pope Sergius the Third had taken a fancy to the celebrated picture and had himself removed it from Saint Mary's, against the wishes of the nuns, to the palace of the Lateran. But the following night, by a miracle, the picture had been returned to the convent. Ever since, the nuns of Saint Mary's had regarded it as beyond all price, and had centered their chief devotions about it. Indeed, there was scarcely one of the present community who had not come to Saint Mary's in order to live under the same roof with the precious relic.

"And since it seems God's Will that the picture remain here, so must we, Father," said Mother Eugenia with an air of finality.

Realizing the uselessness of further argument, Dominic finally took his departure. During his lifetime of fifty years he had been faced with many problems—as a simple priest in Spain, as a missionary among the heretics in southern France, and now as a religious founder in Italy—but certainly this task of reforming the nuns of Rome was as difficult as any. What patience was required! What tact!

"And what prayer!" he said to himself.

The three men whom the Holy Father had assigned as helpers to Dominic in the task of reforming the nuns—Cardinal Ugolino, Cardinal Stephen and Cardinal Nicholas—agreed. In fact, they were inclined to believe that the whole affair was hopeless. As far as they could see, there would never be any unity among the convents in Rome. One community would follow one Rule, one another—and then only as the spirit moved them.

"After all, who can reason with women?" they asked, shrugging their shoulders. "We'd better see if the Holy Father can't release us from this task."

But Dominic did not agree. Well he knew that prayer can accomplish great things. But when penance is added to the prayer, then miracles can be expected. So, as in the days when he had been preaching against the heretics, he turned to the Blessed Mother for help. And to the prayers which he offered to her, he added sacrifices of all kinds— especially fasting.

As he prayed and suffered for the success of this work, Dominic experienced a new and greater love of God. How good He was! How kind! How deserving of the trust and affection of His creatures!

"If I could just make the Sisters understand how much He wants them to serve Him as one family!" he thought. "If I could just get them to realize that the Rule of my children at Prouille, hard though it may be, will help them to become saints. . ."

Then one day a voice spoke in the depths of his soul. *"Why not go to see the Sisters again?"* it whispered. *"Tell them once more that prayer and penance for others can make them truly happy."*

Dominic clasped his hands. The voice within him—hidden, urgent—was surely that of the Holy Spirit! Then what could he do but obey?

CHAPTER 14

THE MIRACLE

D OMINIC'S SECOND VISIT to Saint Mary's was a success. Moved by his words, the nuns realized as never before the emptiness of their spiritual lives, and that thousands of people living in the world were doing far more for God's glory than they. Consider, for instance, the countless men and women who were working long hours, and at difficult tasks, merely to provide the necessities of life for themselves and for their children! Again, consider those other vast numbers—especially those left alone in the world—who were penniless, sick, disabled...

"Father, we've been far too selfish here at Saint Mary's," Mother Eugenia acknowledged. "We've taken everything from God and given Him nothing, for hardly anyone has ever done anything but her own will. But now—well, we'll try to change all that by following the Rule of your Order."

"Yes, Father," put in the other Sisters. "From now on we'll concern ourselves with real prayer and sacrifice for souls."

Of course Dominic was overjoyed at their words, and lost no time in receiving each Sister's promise of obedience. Then he informed the community that within a few days his friars would be ready to leave Saint Sixtus for the new home which Pope Honorius had given them at Santa Sabina. As soon as the move was completed, the Sisters would be free to occupy Saint Sixtus and to accept candidates from other convents who wished to join with them in a holier and more fruitful way of life.

"As for Our Lady's picture, why not bring it with you?" he suggested. "If it returns of its own accord to Saint Mary's—well and good. You will be free to return also."

On February 20 of that year—1220—which was also Ash Wednesday, the nuns of Saint Mary's set out in procession from their home across the Tiber to inspect the recently vacated Monastery of Saint Sixtus. All the bells of Rome were pealing as the little procession moved through the crowded streets—accompanied by Cardinals, Bishops and members of the nobility. And mingled with the sound of the bells was the chorus of thousands of voices, raised in the beautiful hymn to Our Lady which Dominic loved so well:

> Hail, O star of ocean,
> God's own Mother blest,
> Ever sinless Virgin,
> Gate of Heaven's rest.
>
> Taking that sweet Ave
> Which from Gabriel came,

Peace confirm within us,
Changing Eva's name.

Break the sinner's fetters,
To the blind give day,
Ward all evils from us,
For all blessings pray. . .

Dominic's heart was overflowing as he greeted
the procession upon its arrival at Saint Sixtus. How
wonderful it was that Mother Eugenia and her
companions had agreed to live under the new Rule!
Indeed, it was almost like a miracle. For some days
ago, although each Sister had willingly made her
promise of obedience to him in the first place,
there had nevertheless been regrets and doubts on
all sides. Only by the grace of God had Dominic
been able to win the community's confidence once
again.

"Even now, how fearful some of these little ones
are of the cross!" he thought. "And yet, it is only
by accepting it gladly that they will ever have any
real happiness in this life. . ."

Soon the nuns of Saint Mary's, together with the
Cardinals, Bishops and others who had made up
the procession, were seated in the chapter house
of Saint Sixtus—a small building set apart from the
monastery itself. The schedule called for a business
meeting to be held first, at which various details
of the new foundation would be discussed; then the
Holy Sacrifice of the Mass (to be offered by
Dominic), after which all would go in procession
through the monastery and grounds. But the meet-

ing had barely begun when there was a great commotion in the courtyard outside, and an excited messenger rushed in with some dreadful news for Cardinal Stephen—one of Dominic's three advisers. A short distance away Napoleon Orsini, the Cardinal's young nephew, had fallen from his horse and broken his neck!

The Cardinal turned pale. Half rising to his feet, he gripped the breathless messenger by the shoulder. "The boy's not...not *dead*?" he gasped.

"Y-yes, Your Excellency. He died almost at once."

With a great groan the Cardinal sank back in his chair, covering his face with his hands. "Napoleon!" he moaned. "My poor Napoleon..."

Glancing briefly at his friend and adviser, Dominic beckoned to a friar to bring him some Holy Water. Then, having sprinkled the stricken prelate, he asked to be taken without any further delay to the scene of the accident.

"Perhaps all is not lost," he murmured, as if to himself.

However, as Brother Tancred and some of the other friars made ready to accompany him, he shook his head. They could be more useful if they would prepare the altar for Mass. For the time being, the business meeting was postponed. There was a more important kind of "business" to be attended to first.

Napoleon's lifeless body was carried into another room of the chapter house. Then, as soon as everything was ready, Dominic went up to the altar to offer the Holy Sacrifice. And with what fervor he

HE WAS RAISED A PALM'S BREADTH
ABOVE THE GROUND!

said Mass that day! The congregation watched him with increasing awe until, at the solemn moment of the Elevation, a fearful wonder filled every heart.

By some unknown power Dominic was standing about a palm's breadth above the ground, and his face was shining like the sun!

Not the faintest sound could be heard. No one dared to move. Even when the Mass was over, the group in the chapter house remained kneeling silently in their places, as though they had been turned to stone. But Dominic, who had recovered his normal composure, gave no indication that anything extraordinary had happened. Calmly he invited those present to come with him into the room where Napoleon's body was lying.

Scarcely knowing what they did, the assembly obeyed. Then, all being settled, Dominic walked over to the corpse, arranged the stiffening limbs and gave himself over to ardent prayer. With tears streaming down his face, he prostrated himself three times beside the lifeless body, beseeching God to hear his petition.

"Heavenly Father, have mercy upon this poor lad! Have mercy upon him, and deliver him from death . . ."

The minutes passed, and Dominic continued to weep and to pray. Then, taking up his stand by Napoleon's head, he made the Sign of the Cross, and with his hands extended toward Heaven, his body once again raised a palm's breadth above the ground, he cried out in a loud voice:

"Young man, in the Name of Our Lord Jesus Christ—arise!"

At once there was a gasp of astonishment. Slowly, surely, Napoleon was opening his eyes! The next moment he was sitting up, and gazing about the room as though awakening from a deep sleep. Then, his glance falling upon Dominic, he stretched out his arms.

"Father, I'm hungry," he said. "Could I have something to eat and drink?"

Dominic embraced the youth who, but a moment ago, had been dead. "Of course, my son!" he cried joyfully. Then as Cardinal Stephen hastened forward, tears of happy relief coursing down his cheeks, he bade the friars prepare a nourishing meal and bring it at once to the chapter house.

"The lad's alive!" he cried. "God be praised!"

CHAPTER 15

A CALL FROM POLAND

IN A SHORT WHILE word of the miracle had spread throughout Rome, and thousands were flocking to Saint Sixtus to see and speak with the Spanish wonderworker. As for the nuns of Saint Mary's—their fears and scruples about living according to the Rule of Dominic's daughters were now things of the past. How wonderful to be under the guidance of a saint! To have promised obedience to him!

On the following Sunday the solemn inclosure of the nuns took place. There were forty-four to receive the black and white habit of the Order, including a few newcomers and some religious of other convents. Then that same night, accompanied by Cardinals Nicholas, Stephen and some other close friends, all barefoot and with lighted torches in their hands, Dominic carried the Sisters' treasured possession—the picture of Our Lady painted by Saint Luke—to Saint Sixtus.

"If the picture remains here, it will be a sure sign that God is pleased with the new convent," said

Cardinal Nicholas. "But what will you do if it returns, Father Dominic?"

"It won't return, Your Excellency," replied Dominic. "I'm sure of that."

Yet even as this certainty filled his heart, a trace of sorrow crept in also. Just a little while ago the news had reached Santa Sabina that Brother Reginald (who had done so much to promote the Order's welfare in Bologna) had died in the Monastery of Saint James in Paris on February 12, after a brief illness.

"He was only in his early thirties," Dominic reflected. "And we need him so very much! But of course God knows best..."

As he thought about Reginald, recalling how it was to him that the Blessed Mother had presented the scapular of the Order, how Bologna had been "in flames" after his sermons—to quote one of the friars who had worked with him—and that Diana d'Andalò had been converted from a worldly life by his preaching, Dominic's spirits gradually lifted. Reginald was gone, but surely his soul was in glory? Surely in Heaven he would continue to beg God's blessing upon the work of the brethren?

There was another comforting thought. Just a few days before his death, Reginald had received two young Germans into the Order—Brothers Jordan and Henry—who had been studying at the University...

"I remember these young men quite well from my last visit to Paris," Dominic thought, "particularly Jordan. In fact, I can still see the eagerness

on his face as I told him of Brother Reginald's
miraculous cure, of our work, and of my conviction
that God was calling him to be a friar."

Then, recalling Jordan's many fears of the religious life and Henry's complete aversion to it,
Dominic smiled. How wonderful the ways of God!
He, Dominic, had planted the seed; Reginald had
nourished it, and soon would come the harvest. For
certainly Jordan and Henry would do a great work
as preaching friars. Because of their labors, many
souls would be brought to Christ. In fact, deep
within his heart Dominic felt that when he himself
had breathed his last, young Brother Jordan would
be elected to head the Order.

"The boy won't want the work, but it will be his
just the same," he reflected. "And what good he will
do—for the Brothers, the Sisters, and especially for
Diana in Bologna! His letters to her will go down
in history. . ."

A few hours later, however, there were more
pressing matters to claim Dominic's attention than
happy musings about the future. Word was brought
to Santa Sabina that Ivo Odrowatz, recently
appointed Bishop of Cracow, in Poland, desired an
audience with him.

Dominic hastened to greet the Bishop, together
with his priest-nephews, Fathers Ceslaus and Hyacinth, and two lay attendants named Herman and
Henry. He had seen these blue-eyed, fair-haired
strangers from the North before, notably on the
morning when Mother Eugenia and her nuns had
visited Saint Sixtus and young Napoleon Orsini had

met with his accident. In fact, they had been present in the chapter house when the young man had been restored to life.

"Welcome, Your Lordship!" cried Dominic. "This *is* an honor!"

Despite the gracious reception, however, it was evident that none of the newcomers, not even the Bishop, was at ease in Dominic's presence. Hadn't he raised the dead to life, and worked so many other wonders that now his name was a household word throughout all Rome?

For a little while Dominic did most of the talking, while the visitors sat looking at him in awe. But gradually his easy manner captured all hearts, so that the Bishop (plain-spoken and modest by nature) grew eloquent in explaining the reason for his coming. It was because Poland was in such dire need of priests, he said, especially those skilled in preaching. Now if Father Dominic could spare some friars for work in Cracow. . .

"Just three or four of these young men here at Santa Sabina," he said.

"Or. . .or even five or six, Father," Ceslaus added. "You have no idea how much our Northland needs priests."

"Yes," agreed Hyacinth. "The True Faith came to Poland in 965—almost three hundred years ago— but very little progress has been made. Huge numbers of people are still unbaptized."

A shadow crossed Dominic's face as he listened to the visitors' account of the state of the Church in Poland. Apparently there were a few monks in

the country sections and a handful of secular
priests in the cities. Yet Poland covered hundreds
of thousands of square miles, reaching northward
from the Carpathian Mountains to the Baltic Sea
and eastward from Germany to Russia. In this vast
area of forests, plains and valleys, the people were
little more than pagans, and every few years there
were bloody uprisings as the local dukes and barons
made war upon one another.

"You *must* help us, Father!" implored the Bishop.
"Only when the Gospel is preached throughout our
whole country will there be peace."

For a long moment Dominic appeared to consider what had been said. Then slowly he shook his
head.

"Your Lordship, what you ask is impossible," he
replied. Then, as disappointment clouded the prelate's face, he hastened to explain that, despite its
rapid growth in Paris, Rome and Bologna, the
Order of Preachers was really not ready for missionary ventures to pagan lands. Since the beginning, its work had been to fight heresy, especially
in the University cities.

"You see, Your Lordship, when the leaders of the
heretics are converted—and they are usually gifted
men with a University training—then their followers
are like lost sheep. They become an easy prey to
Truth. Hence, this is our mission: to live and work
near the Universities, capture those brilliant minds
which somehow have given themselves to error,
then, through these same minds, to strive to save the
lesser minds which were being led astray."

The Bishop sighed. "I understand, Father," he said. "You and I are both working for souls...but in different ways."

A pang shot through Dominic's heart as the Bishop rose to go. Obviously he had entertained such hopes of securing helpers at Santa Sabina! And now...

Suddenly Dominic was on his feet, too. "Your Lordship, why not give me these young men who have accompanied you here to Rome?" he cried. "In just a little while I would return them to you as experienced workers."

The Bishop stared. "But Father! You can't possibly mean that Ceslaus and Hyacinth..."

"Yes, Your Lordship. I do mean just that. For Poland's sake, give me both your nephews."

The two young priests in question looked at each other. Then suddenly Hyacinth was on his knees, his eyes shining.

"Father, how did you know?" he murmured. "I didn't think that anyone..."

Ceslaus came to kneel beside his younger brother. "You mean it, Father Dominic? You'll really have us in your Order?"

"Yes. And Herman and Henry, too. Come here, my sons."

At once all eyes turned to the two young laymen, simple servants in the episcopal household, who possessed little education and who had never shown any exceptional piety. But now, as Dominic stood beckoning, each hurried forward with child-like eagerness to kneel at his feet.

HERMAN AND HENRY CAME
TO KNEEL AT HIS FEET.

Bishop Ivo wrung his hands. Surely there was some mistake! He had come to Santa Sabina to ask for preaching friars to help with his work in Poland. Instead, both nephews and servants were being taken from him...

"Father..." he began awkwardly, then fell silent. For a lay Brother had suddenly appeared in the doorway, bearing in his arms several white woolen habits. A second Brother followed, carrying holy water and a lighted candle. Then, as a signal was given, the Bishop's four young followers prostrated themselves on the floor in token of their unworthiness to be accepted as God's special servants. A moment later each was being clothed in the habit of the Order, while Dominic prayed aloud in clear and joyful tones:

"Stretch forth, O Lord, unto these Thy servants, the right hand of Thy heavenly assistance, that they may seek Thee with all their hearts, and obtain what they fittingly ask..."

CHAPTER 16

THE WORK IN ROME

W ITHIN A SURPRISINGLY short time
Dominic had convinced Bishop Ivo that
all was not lost. After a brief training
period at Santa Sabina, his nephews and servants
would return to him. And then what wonders the
group would be able to do! Why, they would even
have authority to found new monasteries of preaching friars—to turn the minds of other young men
to the things of God!

"I never thought of that," admitted the Bishop.
"Oh, Father Dominic. . ."

"Yes, Your Lordship?"

"How can I ever thank you for all that you're
doing—for Poland, and for me?"

Dominic smiled. "You could remember me in
your prayers," he said. "That's the best possible gift
any friend can make another."

The Bishop's heart filled with joy at the knowledge that Dominic actually considered him to be
a friend, and he readily promised to keep him in
his prayers. Then, with far greater happiness than

he had ever thought possible, he settled down to await the end of his young followers' training period.

Of course Dominic did not spend all his time at Santa Sabina. Every few days he visited the nuns at Saint Sixtus, encouraging and advising them in their new way of life. And there, of all the community, none awaited his coming more eagerly than did Sister Cecilia, just seventeen years of age, who had been the first to receive the habit from his hands on the day of the solemn inclosure.

"How I wish that I could write his life!" she confided one day to Mother Eugenia. "Or at least some part of it."

The superior looked up with interest. "Well, why not try, child? You have a skill with words."

"You mean I have your permission, Mother?"

"Of course. Some day what you have to say may be of great use."

With great joy Sister Cecilia set about her task—asking questions of this one and that, and making careful note of the answers. Of course much of the information which she gathered was already public knowledge, such as the fact that Father Dominic had been born in Calaroga, Spain, in the year 1170, and that his parents—Don Felix de Guzman and Doña Juana de Aza—were of noble ancestry. But it was not so well-known that he bore the name of Dominic because of his mother's great devotion to Saint Dominic of Sylos, an eleventh-century Abbot of the Benedictine Monastery of Saint Sebastian, not far from Calaroga. There the holy man had

DOÑA JUANA HAD HAD A VISION.

appeared to Doña Juana as she was praying at his tomb (he had then been dead for almost a century), and assured her that her request was granted. She would have a son who would accomplish great things in the apostolate.

There had been another wonderful experience for Doña Juana. Before Saint Dominic's tomb she had had a vision in which she saw a black and white dog with a lighted torch in its mouth running through a darkened world. And as it ran, the torch shone with such brilliance that the shadows melted away and the whole world was filled with light.

"Doña Juana was given to understand that the dog represented her unborn son, the darkness was that of heresy, and the flaming torch the good work of preaching by which some day her son would vanquish ignorance and sin," wrote Sister Cecilia.

There was another wonder to record. At Dominic's Baptism his godmother had seen a heavenly radiance, almost like a star, shining from his forehead. Since then, numerous others claimed to have seen the same thing. Sometimes the light was star-shaped, they said. At other times it was simply an undefined radiance.

"I myself have seen this light," admitted Mother Eugenia, when she read what Sister Cecilia had written. "And it *is* like a star. Haven't you ever noticed it, child?"

Sister Cecilia nodded. "Oh, yes, Mother. Many times. Especially when Father Dominic is talking about God and Heaven."

Naturally there was great interest among the

nuns of Saint Sixtus in Sister Cecilia's project, and
several had suggestions to make concerning "the
book." For instance, what about Father Dominic's
older brothers, Anthony and Mannes? Surely some
mention should be made of them—where they
were and what they were doing?

"They are both in God's service," wrote Sister
Cecilia obligingly. "Anthony is a parish priest in
Spain, and Mannes is a member of our Order and
chaplain of the Sisters at Prouille."

As for Dominic's early miracles, Sister Cecilia
was able to record that the first known of these had
occurred near the French town of Arzens. It had
been on the Feast of Saint John the Baptist in the
year 1206. At that time he had just been beginning
his work among the heretics, and finding that a
number of them were at work in the fields reaping
corn, rather than in church at Mass (it was a Holy
Day in those parts), he tried to show them their
error, assuring them that God would surely punish
their sinfulness. But they only laughed him to
scorn. Then one of the men, who was on the point
of driving Dominic from the field with his sickle,
let out a cry of alarm. The ears of corn which he
had been gathering were stained with blood! And
those of his companions also! As for his hands and
theirs—

"They were dyed a deep and fearful scarlet," Sister Cecilia informed her community. "And so terrified were the men at the sight of their hands, and
the corn, that they fell on their knees at once to

beg Father Dominic's pardon, and to renounce their heresy."

As time went on the young nun redoubled her efforts to find out all that she could of Dominic's life story. What matter if "the book" never materialized? Indeed, if it remained little more than a collection of notes? It was doing her much good to write it. And her community, too.

"I ought to include a description of our good Father, though," she decided one day. "Years from now people will be interested in knowing what he looked like." So after due thought she began to write:

"Father Dominic is of medium height, and rather slightly built. His face is beautiful—with plenty of color. His hair and beard are of a chestnut shade, with a sprinkling of white, and his eyes remarkably fine. From his forehead there seems to shine a radiant light, which draws respect and love from all who see it. He is always joyous and cheerful, save when moved to compassion by the troubles of others. His hands are long and beautifully shaped, his voice clear and musical..."

Of course Dominic knew all about Sister Cecilia's efforts. And he knew something else, too. Some day this young daughter would go to Bologna with another religious from Saint Sixtus—Sister Amata. Here the two would live and work with Diana d'Andalò in establishing the first convent of his nuns in that city. Moreover, centuries later, Sister Cecilia and Sister Amata, like Diana, would be revered as "Blessed" by the entire Order of

Preachers, especially on June 9, their feast day.
"How wonderful!" he often thought. "How truly
wonderful!"

So the days passed—quietly, uneventfully. From
time to time Dominic left his work at Santa Sabina
and Saint Sixtus to preach in various churches. As
usual, he impressed upon his listeners the need for
true confidence in the Blessed Mother. For it was
through her hands that God bestowed all the graces
which Christ had won through His death on
Calvary.

"My children, ask for these graces!" he implored.
"Ask! Ask! Ask! The Blessed Mother never fails to
hear us when we beg her help. . ."

Of course Dominic practiced what he preached,
and not a day passed that he did not seek Our
Lady's blessing upon his work. Then one night,
shortly before the friars were due to assemble for
Matins, the heavenly one showed herself to him
clad in a flowing mantle of sapphire blue. And,
wonder of wonders! Standing beside her was her
Divine Son!

How Dominic rejoiced! Yet even as he looked,
sorrow pierced his heart. Before him were several
other figures—clothed in the habits of various religious Orders. All were gazing upon Our Lord and
His Mother with the utmost love and devotion. But
of his own family there was not one.

Tears began to stream down Dominic's face. How
terrible that no one in the Order of Preachers
should be found worthy to stand in the company
of the Holy Ones! As the thought pressed more

heavily upon him, the Blessed Mother beckoned to him to approach. But his feet were like lead, and only when Our Lord also beckoned to him did he dare draw near, and then merely to prostrate himself in grief.

Suddenly Our Lord spoke. "My son, why do you weep?" He asked.

Dominic scarcely dared to raise his head. "Because I see here religious of all Orders except my own, Lord."

"You would see your own?"

"Y-yes, Lord."

With great tenderness Our Lord placed His right hand upon Our Lady's shoulder. "I have given your Order to My Mother," He said. Then, after a moment's pause: "You would really like to see your children?"

"Oh, yes, Lord!"

At this Our Lady opened her mantle, and Dominic saw the sapphire blue garment slowly spread to cover the whole earth. And there, under its protecting folds, was a vast multitude of men and women, each clad in the black and white habit of his little family!

"Lord, how can I thank You?" cried Dominic, stretching forth his arms. But even as he spoke, the glorious vision faded. He was alone on his knees in the darkness. And. . .and yes—it was time to call the brethren for Matins!

CHAPTER 17

THE WORK CONTINUES

"WE ARE OUR LADY'S children in a special way," said Dominic, when he described the vision to his followers. "She has us under her constant protection."

Great was the rejoicing, not only among the Brothers at Santa Sabina but among the Sisters at Saint Sixtus. How wonderful to know that the Lord had given their family into His Mother's keeping! Presently the first general chapter of the Order was held at Bologna, and to this meeting came delegates from all the convents of preaching friars in France and Spain. The story of the recent apparition was, of course, made known to everyone without delay.

"Our good Father is a saint!" was the word that went from one to another. "Just think! The Lord comes to console and strengthen him!"

"Yes. And Our Lady, too!"

"But before long he'll have no need of that."

"*No need?*"

"Haven't you noticed how his health is failing?"

"Oh, no!"

"It's true. One of these days Our Lord and His Mother will come to him for the last time. They'll take him to Heaven."

The rumor concerning Dominic's failing health spread quickly.

"Nonsense!" cried Dominic when he heard it. "The Lord will leave me on earth as long as I am needed. Never fear."

"But you do look tired, Father," Brother Humbert insisted. "Surely if you rested more, and ate more nourishing food..."

Dominic shook his head. "I'm quite all right," he said. "Believe me, these days there isn't time to be sick."

Gradually the friars allowed themselves to be persuaded that all was well. As Dominic moved among them at the general chapter, cheerful and eager, ever willing to listen to the troubles of others, and especially to impress upon the weaker brethren that the Rule of the Order was meant to be a help to happiness, not a hindrance, and that it did not bind under pain of sin, they set aside their fears.

"Father Dominic is in good health after all," they said. "Thank God!"

"Yes. He's only fifty years old. He'll be with us for a long time yet."

Dominic was greatly relieved that his health was no longer a cause for concern, and when it was decided to undertake a campaign against the Albigenses in northern Italy, he was among the first to offer his services. And as he prayed and preached, an attractive idea—although not a new one—presented itself. He would extend membership in his Order to people living in the world!

"We need the help of the laity in our work," he thought, "just as we did in southern France during the war against Count Raymond."

Presently Dominic and his missionaries were urging zealous laymen to offer themselves for the defense of the Church against the heretics. They would be known as the Militia of Jesus Christ and would wear white tunics and black mantles, with the black and white cross of the Order of Preachers. Every day they would recite a certain number of Our Fathers and Hail Marys, and in return for their services they would share in the good works of the entire Order.

Of course Dominic made it plain that the members of the Militia were never to be cruel in warfare, or to give themselves to bloodshed without a just cause. The sole reason for the group's existence was that it might serve as a protective force, spiritually as well as physically. It was to take up the sword only when Catholics and their property were threatened by the heretics.

During the months which followed, the preaching campaign in northern Italy produced many conversions. The work of the Militia of Jesus Christ was also successful, and Dominic's heart filled with joy. Deep within himself he felt that the battle against heresy was slowly being won—in France as well as in Italy. The countless Hail Marys said in Our Lady's honor were having their effect, and surely before many years had passed the Albigenses would no longer menace the Christian world.

"When that day comes, the Militia of Jesus Christ will have a new name," he thought. "It will be 'The Order of Penance,' to which women may belong as well as men."

It never occurred to Dominic that some day the group would be better known by quite another name—the secular Third Order of Saint Dominic; and that it would be found in all parts of the world, producing saints for Heaven. He was more concerned in making plans for the second general chapter of the Order, to be held at Bologna within a few weeks' time, than in speculations about the distant future.

"What a meeting this is going to be!" he thought with satisfaction. "How many important decisions will be made!"

When the friars assembled at Bologna on May 30, 1221, for their second general chapter, there were indeed many pressing matters to be discussed. And at the top of the list was the question of sending competent preachers to distant lands.

"Let me go to England, Father!" begged Brother Gilbert, who had come from that country some years ago to study law at the University of Bologna. "I know that I could do good there."

"And let me go to Hungary," urged Brother Paul, who also had left his native land to attend the University.

"Father Dominic, I think that I could be of use in Denmark," put in Brother Solomon. "And in

THE BISHOP DID NOT APPROVE
OF BEGGING FRIARS.

other parts of the Northland, too."

"I could work in Greece, Father..."

"I could work in Germany..."

"I know English, Father. Let me go with Brother Gilbert!"

"And me!"

"And me!"

Dominic looked with satisfaction on the eager faces of his sons. Apostles, every one of them! And on fire with zeal! How splendid that they wanted to go forth with the message of the True Faith—especially to England! For surely there was a wonderful field there for preachers and teachers of the Word of God? Even in Italy it was common knowledge that the little town of Oxford was fast becoming an important center of learning. In a few years its schools might rival those of Paris and Bologna.

Soon there was another cause for rejoicing. Bishop Conrad of Porto, the apostolic legate in Bologna, had never really approved the work of Dominic's little family. Cautious by nature, he was suspicious of all new movements in the Church, and the sight of youthful friars preaching in the streets in their black and white habits, even begging their bread from door to door, filled him with alarm. Surely boys who had embraced the religious life ought to remain in the cloister, rather than endanger their vocations by spending so much time among men and women of the world. Then one day during the second general chapter...

"Bishop Conrad's now our friend!" Brother Peter announced joyfully to the assembled friars. "He's much in favor of the way we work!"

The other friars could scarcely believe their ears. "What's happened?" they wanted to know. "What made the Bishop change his mind?"

Brother Peter lost no time in explaining. Just a little while ago the Bishop, still worried about the way in which Dominic's young helpers were going about their work, had begged God to enlighten him. Was the Order of Preachers really a good thing? Was it right to criticize Father Dominic for allowing his disciples to preach in the streets and attend the classes at the University?

"The Bishop prayed, then called for a Missal to be brought to him," Brother Peter told the community. "Then he opened it, and placed his finger on the first words he saw. And what do you suppose they were?"

"What?"

"Laudare, benedicere, praedicare!"

At once a murmur of excitement ran through the little group. "To praise, to bless, to preach!" Why, Father Dominic had often used these very words (taken from the Preface of the Mass of the Blessed Virgin) to explain the work which he and his followers were trying to do! And of course the Bishop knew this. . .

Dominic was just as pleased as anyone over this approval of his work from an unexpected quarter, and when the general chapter ended and he set out for Venice to visit his old friend, Cardinal Ugolino, the three Latin words—*laudare, benedicere, praedicare*—kept up a joyful rhythm in his heart.

"To praise, to bless, to preach!" he said to himself over and over again. "Why, it's the perfect motto for our little family!" Then, after a moment's thought: "And so is another word—*Veritas!*"

Yes, *Veritas,* or "Truth," had been the real reason for the Order's birth. Through the years, and in various places, the Devil had made use of heresy in his efforts to drag souls to Hell. Knowing that ignorance is the breeding place for evil, he had done his best to foster it in the hearts of the people. And he had succeeded all too well, for never had there been a trained body of preachers and teachers to go out and fight against him. But now—in France and Spain and Italy...in Germany, Hungary, England...

"Dearest Mother, continue to bless our work!" whispered Dominic. "And pray for us sinners, now and at the hour of our death..."

CHAPTER 18

BOLOGNA AGAIN

HIS VISIT WITH Cardinal Ugolino at an end, Dominic left Venice and returned to Bologna. But even as he made the trip, stopping to preach in towns along the way, he knew that his days were almost over. The fever which had come upon him during the first and second general chapters had returned. How tired he was! How weak!

"It's the heat, Father," said Brother Ventura, the Prior. "July is always a bad month in Bologna."

But Dominic shook his head. "On the sixth day of August. . . the Feast of the Transfiguration. . ."

"Yes, Father? What about that day?"

"I shall die then, Brother. Here in your city."

Tears sprang to Brother Ventura's eyes. "Oh, no, Father! Why, you're only fifty-one years old! You can't leave us for a long time yet!"

But as the days passed, the Prior was forced to recognize that Father Dominic *was* ill—mortally ill. In a week, possibly two. . .

Grief filled every heart at the Monastery of Saint

Nicholas in Bologna. What would happen to the Order of Preachers, scarcely five years old, when its founder should have gone home to God? Who would supervise the work? Who would plan, encourage, console, advise?

"There just isn't anyone to take Father Dominic's place," the brethren said despairingly. "He's a saint. There's not another like him in the whole world."

Then their hopes were raised somewhat when someone suggested that Dominic might be saved by a miracle. "After all, look at the miracles he has worked for others."

"That's right. At least three times he's raised the dead to life."

"And he's had the gift of tongues, too. Why, once he traveled with some German pilgrims for four days, and they understood every word he said to them!"

"Yes. And remember what happened in Fanjeaux?"

"You mean when Father Dominic was trying to convert the leaders of the heretics?"

"Yes. They accepted his challenge to throw the manuscript of their speeches into a fire—as a test of truth."

"And the flames consumed the pages at once!"

"But when Father Dominic threw in his speech..."

"It flew back into his hands unharmed."

"Not once, but three times."

Over and over again the brethren tried to console themselves by relating other wonders in Dominic's life. But finally they realized that it was not God's Will that Dominic should work miracles for himself. His days were numbered. They must resign themselves to the fact that soon he would leave them forever.

"Don't worry," Dominic told his little family more than once, noting the tense and sorrowful faces. "In Heaven I shall be of much more use to you than I am now."

With this the brethren tried to be content, but in Rome—one hundred and eighty miles to the southeast—the Sisters at Saint Sixtus and the Brothers at Santa Sabina were almost beside themselves with grief. Never to see their beloved father again! Not even to have his body rest among them!

"He was so kind!" sobbed Mother Eugenia. "So fatherly! Remember when he came back from a preaching trip and brought each of us a spoon as a souvenir?"

"Yes. And those wonderful times, after the day's work was over, when he came for a visit!"

"How beautifully he spoke to us then about God's love and mercy!"

"And about the Blessed Mother!"

"It was like listening to an angel!"

"Or to Christ Himself!"

As they went about their prayers and labors in the monastery which Dominic himself had designed, the brethren of Santa Sabina were as grief-stricken as the nuns. But like the Sisters and the friars in Bologna, they tried to find comfort in recalling past events in their beloved father's life.

For instance, here was the altar where he had offered the Holy Sacrifice with such devotion. Over there was the place where the Blessed Mother had appeared to him, her sapphire blue cloak encircling the entire Order. Outside in the garden was the little orange tree which he had planted only a few months ago. . .

"Come back, Father!" pleaded Brother Tancred, whose office of Prior weighed more heavily than ever, now that he knew that never again in this world would he see the face of his superior. "Don't leave us alone!"

But it was not only at Saint Sixtus and Santa Sabina that hearts were heavy. Thousands of lay people were shocked and grieved by the news of Dominic's mortal illness. How much he had done for them by his sermons and friendly visits! How many had found a new joy in life because of his advice and encouragement—especially the suggestion that they recite the Hail Mary frequently and devoutly, and so come to a better knowledge and love of the Blessed Mother!

"*Hail Mary, full of grace.* . .who could ever say that little prayer more beautifully than Father Dominic?"

"Or who could preach such sermons?"

"No wonder the Pope made him Master of the Sacred Palace—the chief preacher and teacher at the Vatican."

Dominic was well aware of the people's sorrow, and repeated what he had already told his friars: that he would be of much more use to souls in

Heaven than he had ever been on earth. But early in August, seeing that they were not yet reconciled to his death, he consented to be taken from the Monastery of Saint Nicholas in Bologna to a hill outside the city where there was a little shrine to Our Lady. It was cooler there, and perhaps he might survive a few days longer.

However, in just a short while the brethren were filled with dismay. They had discovered that the priest in charge of Our Lady's shrine intended to put forth a claim to have their beloved father's body buried there. Moreover, he would be within his rights.

"It can't be!" cried Brother Moneta. "Father Dominic belongs with us. . .at Saint Nicholas!"

"But if we take him back into the heat of the city. . ."

"We can't do that! He'd die right away!"

"He might even die before we got home!"

"Mother of God, what shall we do?"

In the end it was decided to place the whole matter before Father Dominic. And without delay he gave his answer. "Take me back to Saint Nicholas!" he begged. "God forbid that I should be buried anywhere save under the feet of my brethren!"

Sorrowing, the little group prepared to carry the dying man back into the city. By now his breath was coming in labored gasps, and it seemed as though each one might be his last. But he continued to cling to life.

"Courage, my sons," he whispered, a smile playing about his pain-racked features. "All is well. . ."

Throughout the trip into the city, sorrowing crowds pressed forward to catch a last glimpse of him. This was Father Dominic de Guzman, one of the holiest men in all Europe. And he was going home to his monastery to die!

"Father, give us your blessing!" they cried, falling to their knees.

"Pray for us, Father. . ."

"Don't forget us when you go to Heaven. . ."

Repeatedly Dominic raised his hand in blessing, still with the smile upon his lips. "My friends," he murmured. "My good friends. . ."

But when at last the brethren arrived at the doors of Saint Nicholas, he closed his eyes and sank back.

"The trip was too much for him," said Brother Ventura. "He's. . .he's dying right now!"

"No, it's just the heat."

"But he can scarcely breathe!"

Carefully the friars carried Dominic into the monastery and to the cell of Brother Moneta, since he did not have a cell of his own. Then, with gentle hands, they removed the habit which he had been wearing and replaced it with a fresh one belonging to Brother Moneta.

"He doesn't even have a bed of his own with us—or an extra habit!" whispered the Prior. "He, who's given us everything!"

Suddenly Dominic made a faint motion. "Begin the prayers. . ." he murmured.

At once the community gathered close about the

bedside, prepared to recite the prayers for the dying. But without warning Dominic opened his eyes. "Wait a moment," he said. Then, with sudden strength: "I am going where I can serve you better."

There was silence, with now and then a muffled sob. Father Dominic was sinking fast! He who, after reviewing the years past, had revealed that God had preserved him in perfect purity his whole life long. He who had left to his spiritual sons this last testament: "Have charity among you; hold to humility; keep willing poverty."

"Father. . . Father. . ."

Once again a smile crossed Dominic's face. Then he motioned feebly with his hand. "Begin," he said, and closed his eyes.

In choked voices the community began the prayers for the dying, led by Brother Ventura.

"We commend to Thee, O Lord, the soul of Thy servant. . . may the heavens be opened unto him and the angels rejoice with him. . . may the holy angels of God come out to meet him, and conduct him into the heavenly Jerusalem. . ."

"Come to his assistance, all ye saints of God; meet him, all ye angels of God; receive his soul, and present it now before its Lord. . ."

Suddenly Brother Ventura stopped. "Look!" he whispered unbelievingly.

The friars leaned forward. Dominic had stopped breathing! And about his head was an unearthly radiance—shaped like a star—which seemed to grow brighter even as they gazed upon it.

"HE LIVES—NOW AND FOREVER!"

"He's dead!" gasped Brother Moneta.

"He *lives!*" said Brother Ventura joyfully. "Now and forever!"

St. Meinrad, Indiana
Feast of the Ascension of Our Lord
May 6, 1948

Also by the same author . . .

6 <u>MORE</u> GREAT CATHOLIC BOOKS FOR CHILDREN

. . . and for all young people ages 10 to 100!!

1200 SAINT THOMAS AQUINAS—The Story of "The Dumb Ox." 81 pp. PB. 16 Illus. Impr. The remarkable story of how St. Thomas, called in school "The Dumb Ox," became the greatest Catholic teacher ever.　　6.00

1201 SAINT CATHERINE OF SIENA—The Story of the Girl Who Saw Saints in the Sky. 65 pp. PB. 13 Illus. The amazing life of the most famous Catherine in the history of the Church.　　5.00

1202 SAINT HYACINTH OF POLAND—The Story of The Apostle of the North. 189 pp. PB. 16 Illus. Impr. Shows how the holy Catholic Faith came to Poland, Lithuania, Prussia, Scandinavia and Russia.　　11.00

1203 SAINT MARTIN DE PORRES—The Story of The Little Doctor of Lima, Peru. 122 pp. PB. 16 Illus. Impr. The incredible life and miracles of this black boy who became a great saint.　　7.00

1204 SAINT ROSE OF LIMA—The Story of The First Canonized Saint of the Americas. 132 pp. PB. 13 Illus. Impr. The remarkable life of the little Rose of South America.　　8.00

1205 PAULINE JARICOT—Foundress of the Living Rosary and The Society for the Propagation of the Faith. 244 pp. PB. 21 Illus. Impr. The story of a rich young girl and her many spiritual adventures.　　13.00

1206 ALL 6 BOOKS·ABOVE (Reg. 50.00)　　　　THE SET: 40.00

Prices guaranteed through December 31, 1998.

U.S. & CAN. POST./HDLG.: $1-$10, add $2; $10.01-$20, add $3; $20.01-$30, add $4; $30.01-$50, add $5; $50.01-$75, add $6; $75.01-up, add $7.

At your Bookdealer or direct from the Publisher.
Call Toll Free 1-800-437-5876

More books by the same author . . .

8 <u>MORE</u> GREAT CATHOLIC BOOKS FOR CHILDREN

. . . and for all young people ages 10 to 100!!

1230 SAINT PAUL THE APOSTLE—The Story of the Apostle to the Gentiles. 231 pp. PB. 23 Illus. Impr. The many adventures that met St. Paul in the early Catholic Church. 13.00

1231 SAINT BENEDICT—The Story of the Father of the Western Monks. 158 pp. PB. 19 Illus. Impr. The life and great miracles of the man who planted monastic life in Europe. 8.00

1232 SAINT MARGARET MARY—And the Promises of the Sacred Heart of Jesus. 224 pp. PB. 21 Illus. Impr. The wonderful story of remarkable gifts from Heaven. Includes St. Claude de la Colombière. 11.00

1233 SAINT DOMINIC—Preacher of the Rosary and Founder of the Dominican Order. 156 pp. PB. 19 Illus. Impr. The miracles, trials and travels of one of the Church's most famous saints. 8.00

Continued on next page . . .

1234 KING DAVID AND HIS SONGS—A Story of the Psalms. 138 pp. PB. 23 Illus. Impr. The story of the shepherd boy who became a warrior, a hero, a fugitive, a king, and more.   8.00

1235 SAINT FRANCIS SOLANO—Wonder-Worker of the New World and Apostle of Argentina and Peru. 205 pp. PB. 19 Illus. Impr. The story of St. Francis' remarkable deeds in Spain and South America.   11.00

1236 SAINT JOHN MASIAS—Marvelous Dominican Gatekeeper of Lima, Peru. 156 pp. PB. 14 Illus. Impr. The humble brother who fought the devil and freed a million souls from Purgatory.   8.00

1237 BLESSED MARIE OF NEW FRANCE—The Story of the First Missionary Sisters in Canada. 152 pp. PB. 18 Illus. Impr. The story of a wife, mother and nun—and her many adventures in pioneer Canada.   9.00

1238 ALL 8 BOOKS ABOVE (Reg. 76.00)   THE SET: 60.00

Prices guaranteed through December 31, 1998.

Get the Complete Set!! . . .

SET OF ALL 20 TITLES

by Mary Fabyan Windeatt

(Individually priced—179.00   Reg. set prices—143.00)

1256 THE SET OF ALL 20 . . . . Only 125.00

U.S. & CAN. POST./HDLG.: $1-$10, add $2; $10.01-$20, add $3; $20.01-$30, add $4; $30.01-$50, add $5; $50.01-$75, add $6; $75.01-up, add $7.

At your Bookdealer or direct from the Publisher.
Call Toll Free 1-800-437-5876

TAN BOOKS AND PUBLISHERS, INC.
P.O. Box 424
Rockford, Illinois 61105

MARY FABYAN WINDEATT

Mary Fabyan Windeatt could well be called the "storyteller of the saints," for such indeed she was. And she had a singular talent for bringing out doctrinal truths in her stories, so that without even realizing it, young readers would see the Catholic catechism come to life in the lives of the saints.

Mary Fabyan Windeatt wrote at least 21 books for children, plus the text of about 28 Catholic story coloring books. At one time there were over 175,000 copies of her books on the saints in circulation. She contributed a regular "Children's Page" to the monthly Dominican magazine, *The Torch*.

Miss Windeatt began her career of writing for the Catholic press around age 24. After graduating from San Diego State College in 1934, she had gone to New York looking for work in advertising. Not finding any, she sent a story to a Catholic magazine. It was accepted—and she continued to write. Eventually Miss Windeatt wrote for 33 magazines, contributing verse, articles, book reviews and short stories.

Having been born in 1910 in Regina, Saskatchewan, Canada, Mary Fabyan Windeatt received the Licentiate of Music degree from Mount Saint Vincent College in Halifax, Nova Scotia at age 17. With her family she moved to San Diego in that same year, 1927. In 1940 Miss Windeatt received an A.M. degree from Columbia University. Later, she lived with her mother near St. Meinrad's Abbey, St. Meinrad, Indiana. Mary Fabyan Windeatt died on November 20, 1979.

(Much of the above information is from Catholic Authors: Contemporary Biographical Sketches 1930-1947, *ed. by Matthew Hoehn, O.S.B., B.L.S., St. Mary's Abbey, Newark, N.J., 1957.)*